CONFIDENT PUBLIC SPEAKING

How to Communicate Effectively Using the PowerTalk System

Christian H. Godefroy & Stephanie Barrat

PIATKUS

Other books by Christian Godefroy published by Piatkus

The Complete Time Management System (with John Clark)
The Outstanding Negotiator (with Luis Robert)
Mind Power (with D. R. Steevens)
Super Health

First published in Great Britain in 1991 by
Judy Piatkus (Publishers) Limited of
5 Windmill Street, London W1P 1HF

First paperback edition 1993
This revised edition published in 1998

The moral right of the authors has been asserted

Originally published as *The Power Talk System*

A catalogue record for this book is available from the British Library

ISBN 0-7499-1827-6

Printed and bound in Great Britain by
Butler & Tanner Ltd, Frome and London

CONTENTS

PART THREE: **How to use professional techniques – and succeed!**

INTRODUCING
THE POWER TALK SYSTEM

When you observe some politicians, or some stars on TV, don't you have a secret admiration for their poise and self-confidence? Wouldn't you like to be able to go in front of the cameras with their naturalness and self-confidence?

Do not think that their skills are born gifts. These men and women have known stage-fright. They were once scared to express themselves. However, they were able to attain their positions of power or success because they worked on this problem. They followed courses and learned public speaking techniques and communication skills.

You can do the same. Quietly, without leaving your home, you can improve your self-confidence and master the art of public speaking. This book synthesises all researches in that field. *The Power Talk System* is the method used by effective communicators and forms the basis of our courses and seminars on confident speaking.

- It will give you confidence to speak in front of others.

- It will help you to overcome stage-fright.

- It will enable you to express your ideas more clearly and precisely.

- It will help you with your studies.

- It will make you communicate more effectively at interviews and meetings.

- It will improve your presentation skills.

- It will give you the edge when you appear on radio and television.

What is the Power Talk System?

The *Power Talk System* – or PTS, to give it the modern look it deserves – is based on the idea that expressing yourself well gives you power, and that this is something you can learn.

The Power Talk System can provide you with years of experience, and help you discover new ideas and rules that have been proven effective. Our approach is practical and methodical. There is a constant interaction between the reader and the authors. You are forced to think, to discover things for yourself, and to adapt the method to your own life and needs. Also, you 'direct' your own training programme, adjusting it to your personal rhythm. You can go back and review a portion of the text, pick out what is most useful to you personally. Many people who have followed our course have told us that the method has become like a faithful friend which helps them progress, step by step, towards becoming effective communicators.

PTS has a very original structure: one idea per chapter, each chapter designed according to the rules of good communication, with an introduction, visual aids, reader participation, practical support files, etc. It is the most complete and practical method we have encountered.

The basic structure differs from the traditional 'schoolroom' style. Instead of restricting readers by placing them in a rigid mould, we encourage them to break out of the straitjacket that prevents them from being themselves. The potential to be an effective communicator is already there, in each and every one of us. The problem is getting it out. And that's exactly what the Power Talk System does.

The importance of communication today

After centuries of living in a predominantly agrarian society, followed by the industrial revolution where the main thing was to *produce*, we have now entered the age of communication. Company leaders and their executives, according to a recent U.S. study, spend 85 per cent of their time communicating.

Communicating your ideas, convincing people, negotiating a contract, motivating personnel, all these activities depend on oral expression. And oral expression is just as important in people's social and personal lives. Too many people are incapable of expressing what they think and feel.

Fear of communicating, or suppressing what you want to say, is the cause of a host of psychological problems. But by far the most important aspect is that through oral expression you also learn to communicate with yourself, to accept yourself and become a happier person.

By liberating your gestures, you often liberate your brain as well, and the ideas start flowing. The Power Talk System places a lot of emphasis on body language. It is a method of personal development, designed from a professional standpoint, whose sole objective is to improve the effectiveness of communication.

You can no longer hide behind your desk

Public speaking has made a strong comeback. The explosion of local radio and satellite television stations is part of the phenomenon. Access to public networks by private enterprise is expanding. According to a communications specialist, Heinz Goldman, 'Bosses and executives can no longer hide behind their desks.'

Often managers are turning to the media in order to increase their companies' revenues by talking to the public direct. This needs confidence and good communication skills.

Unions, which have long been aware of trends, offer their delegates courses in public speaking. The renewed interest in communication also benefits employers: why permit personnel to go on strike when the problems could be solved in a well-organised meeting, or a series of discussions?

Politicians have, more than ever, to face the public on and off camera. Their comments, debates, speeches and meetings are recorded, amplified and analysed by journalists.

Aspiring or inexperienced politicians lose a lot of sleep over the speeches they have to deliver the next day. Many of them suffer from stage-fright, which deprives them of a vital source of energy, and makes their performances less than convincing. 'The demand for oral expression courses has never been as strong as it is today,' declares an expert in the field.

Another situation where oral expression – and stage-fright – are of primary importance is in job interviews.

Multinationals use a technique of placing candidates for executive positions together in simulated meetings. You reply to an advertisement and, if you're considered qualified enough, you find yourself in a group with 15 other candidates, being analysed by the attentive eyes of psychologists and human-resource specialists.

In so many situations, the person who speaks best has a considerable advantage over others, and usually ends up way ahead in the game of promotions and success. This is a new phenomenon. True, in the middle ages the art of public speaking was systematically taught to the nobility; true, hardly a century ago rhetoric was part of every student's curriculum. But with the arrival of universal education programmes education in public speaking declined and was eventually eliminated completely.

Once a symbol of power and wealth, rhetorical skill became derided and forgotten. Which is unfortunate for us, since in the modern world the inability to communicate is a considerable handicap which almost everyone, from executives to craftsmen, has to overcome.

Who will benefit from the Power Talk System method?

Our clientele is very varied. That is what is so interesting about this kind of work. We train students who haven't yet learned to communicate, and who are afraid of their oral exams. We train unemployed people who want to do well in their job interviews. Heads of companies, trades people. People starting their own businesses, who have to talk to bankers, suppliers, customers. Doctors, dentists, lawyers, notaries. Also a lot of people who work in communication – radio and television personalities, journalists, politicians. They all know that, as John D. Rockefeller said:

> 'The ability to come to an understanding with people – the ability to communicate – is something that can be bought, just like you'd buy sugar or coffee. And I'm willing to pay more for this quality than for anything else under the sun!'

People need to know what to say and how to say it, and how to say the right thing at the right time. The words of the President of Chrysler, Lee Iacocca, ring true:

> 'An executive who can't get along with people is crippled. It's a deadly fault. Because everything he does involves other people. He doesn't work with dogs or monkeys – just people. And if he can't get along with his peers, then what can he be expected to do for the company? His role as an executive is to motivate others. If he can't do that, then he has no place with us.'

The greatest speakers weren't *born* speakers – they *became* speakers

Everyone who speaks well in public makes it look like it's a natural talent. It's the same thing with dancing. What appears natural – and has become natural − is the result of hours of study and effort. The greatest speakers weren't *born* speakers − they *became* speakers. Winston Churchill was a terrible orator when he started out. Charles de Gaulle worked for years on his delivery. François Mitterand failed his orals at university because of stage-fright.

Learning to speak is a little like the piano. Not everyone can be a virtuoso, but almost anyone can have fun playing and reach a certain level of proficiency. It's just a question of training.

And the Power Talk System makes the training easy, by incorporating techniques of mental suggestion and subconscious psychology.

Communicating is so important for human beings that even if you are 'gifted' the gift is worth improving. And if you don't think you're gifted, then this method is a necessity!

We still have moments of stage-fright − and are happy about it. It's a signal, and it's a fantastic storehouse of energy. What disturbs most people who experience stage-fright is its *paralysing effect*. But with PTS you learn to channel the energy these stress hormones produce and *transform* it into a power of conviction, into enthusiasm. In other words, you learn how to gather all these scattered forces into a single, controlled flow of energy that actually improves communication.

The Power Talk System also shows you how not to let stage-fright develop when it isn't necessary. You can control stage-fright at will. A lot of people are really surprised at how easy it is to do this – to channel your energy – when you know how.

How the Power Talk System will affect your whole life

The effect that PTS has on a person's overall personality never fails to amaze us. This is probably what is most fascinating about the method, and about our work. You can't imagine to what point people are transformed once they have learned to control their emotions and express themselves with ease. It's as if all their potential were suppressed behind a barrier − the fear of expressing themselves. Open the barrier, and although they may still be using only 10 per cent of their potential, they become themselves, and acquire the confidence they were lacking in their own abilities.

There is life *before* PTS and life *after* PTS.

After the Power Talk System a person dares to assume his or her rightful place in society, dares to take risks, dares to express ideas and opinions and to live a full, rewarding life. For many executives, this a crucial stage in their career.

This is what motivated us to share the techniques we discovered. Of all methods of personal development, oral expression is the strongest and most profound means for progressing that we know about. It's fun, and it really does change your life.

PART 1

How to improve your communication skills – and liberate your potential

CHAPTER 1

EXPLOIT YOUR ASSETS

'In the same way that genius is the fruit of long perseverance, eloquence is something you learn. The great advantage of the Power Talk System is that it's marvellously adapted to the accelerated pace of our times.'
MARK FISHER, best-selling business author

Mastering the spoken word: the key to self-confidence

Being able to stay calm when dealing with problems, mobilising reserves of mental and physical energy when the need arises – many of the qualities that make a person a 'winner' – are developed through oral expression training. Expressing yourself in public and overcoming your fears is one of the keys to self-confidence.

'Since I learned to express myself in front of people without difficulty, my relations with other people have been completely transformed,' states a young executive. 'I no longer hesitate to express my ideas, to respond to criticism and to defend my opinions until I succeed.'

It is true that the fear of speaking in public has always been a part of people's psychological make-up. Overcoming this fear makes us aware of the enormous creative and innovative potential that we all possess: a potential that can be expressed only once we are liberated from the emotional forces which block communication.

But in order to achieve your potential you need to be confident in your abilities.

How is your self-confidence in front of the public? What are your good points and bad points as a communicator?

Your qualities as a communicator

Out of the hundreds of executives who have attended our conferences, only between 15 and 20 per cent had anything good to say about their qualities as communicators – and this despite the fact that to have got where they were, to live and survive, being able to communicate was essential.

You *already know* how to communicate. But you're like a radio station that isn't quite tuned in to the right wavelength. It crackles, there's interference, but despite all the noise just a slight adjustment will get it working perfectly.

So now it's your turn. You've been forewarned. You *do have* communication qualities. They are your most important assets. They are the foundation on which the Power Talk System is built. So take ten minutes, and note down your virtues and your faults as a communicator.

GOOD POINTS	ASPECTS TO IMPROVE

Finished already? Let's see: did you mention the way you *look at people*, your *voice*, your *attitude*, your *body language*, your *gestures*, how *clearly* you speak, the *progression of your ideas*, your *knowledge of psychology*, your *power of conviction*, the way you *listen to others*, how well you *understand them?*

Do you know how to *use examples*, how to *keep your sentences short?*

Do you take enough *time* to explain yourself while knowing when to be *short and concise?*

Do you adapt *the way you dress* to the circumstances?

Do you *prepare yourself physically?* Mentally?

Do you prepare a *plan?*

Do you set your *objectives* before speaking?

Do you know *when to stop?*

Do you know how *to ask questions?*

Do you speak with *authority?*

Are you *really interested* in others? Do you encourage them to speak with nods of the head, looks, reassuring phrases like 'Oh yes . . .' 'Of course . . .' 'Exactly . . .' 'I agree . . .'

Do you *smile* (with your mouth, your eyes . . .)?

Do you make sure that your listeners have fully *understood* you?

Can you deliver a speech with *punch?*

Are you *sincere? Natural? Sensitive?*

Do you know how to *take advantage of circumstances?*

Do you have a sense of *timing?* Can you *improvise? Tell funny stories?*

Are you *calm?* Are you *attractive? Tolerant?*

Do you know how to *respond to criticism?* Do you *capture attention* right from the start?

Go ahead – take another five minutes and really get into it. Try to see yourself in your recent conversations, in the situations where you've had to communicate, and examine your qualities, and the things you'd like to change.

Now take each item and look at its opposite. Let us explain: there are the virtues of your faults, and the faults of your virtues. For example, if you know how to *listen to others* (+), then maybe you *let people walk all over you* and have problems expressing your own ideas and interrupting when you think you should (−). If you're *calm* (+), then you *lack enthusiasm* (−).

It's very important, in this exercise, to concentrate on transforming faults into virtues:

- Stage-fright can be seen as a virtue of sensitivity, and as a gift for expressing your *emotions.*
- *Not standing still* can be seen as a virtue when compared with someone who is frozen in one place.
- Not knowing how to make *small talk* is a virtue in itself!
- Not smiling can, in certain cases, create the right impression of being '*serious about things*'.
- Not being prepared can create a tone of *authenticity.*
- Being aggressive can add *punch.*

And so on.

Maybe you think that to be a good communicator you have to pattern yourself after some ideal model, follow unbending rules and 'fit the mould', so to speak.

That's one way of seeing things but that's not our opinion. We can recognise a Dale Carnegie graduate right away. He's *forcing himself*. He has to *make an effort* to do the things he thinks are necessary, and that's not natural. In fact, it's exactly the opposite of what should be happening.

Instead of imposing more restrictions, the Power Talk System liberates the natural faculties of expression. It's just like a sculptor who, instead of adding material, works by removing from the block everything that isn't necessary, until the perfect form is achieved.

What we are saying is that it's our own mental blocks, our fears, our apprehensions, which prevent us from communicating effectively. And it's by learning how to free ourselves from these shackles that we can attain real self-expression, because everything we need is already inside us – at least potentially.

The only limits on our accomplishments of tomorrow are the doubts we have today. So let's examine these doubts, these fears, and see how we can get rid of them.

CHAPTER 2

HOW TO OVERCOME THE FEAR OF OTHERS

'You don't run away because you're afraid. You're afraid because you run away from your fear.'

WILLIAM JAMES, psychologist

Steven Spielberg, millionaire film-maker, with of a string of blockbuster hits such as *Jaws*, *Close Encounters of the Third Kind*, *E.T.*, *Raiders of the Lost Ark*, etc., declares:

'My greatest fear is speaking in public. Fear of insects takes second place. I remember, during a conference I was giving to students of American law, completely forgetting how to speak English, my mother tongue! I started trying to think in French. It only lasted a minute or two, but it was terrifying!'

Have you ever experienced this kind of panic bred from fear? Have you ever had to express yourself in front of others, only to find that you've lost all your faculties? Or are you just *afraid of being placed in such a situation one day?*

Fear is the result of ignorance and uncertainty. One way of not being afraid of your fear is to become familiar with it and understand it.

How fear arises – and how to avoid it

Fear, which can assume a number of forms (apprehension, stage-fright, anxiety, tension, nervousness) is a *preparation for action*.

The mechanism works as follows:

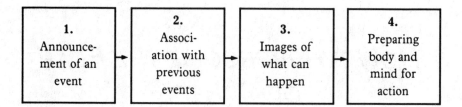

Where does fear enter into this process?

Your answer: _____

The correct answer: The emotion of fear begins with stage 2: association with previous events.

Most people try to work on stage 4. Their blood vessels are already transporting quantities of stress hormones. Their hearts are pumping like mad. They sweat, they're feverish or cold − or both. There are ways to control the effects of this fear, known as stage-fright, which we'll see later on.

The most advanced methods, such as positive thinking, suggest tackling stage 3, creating reassuring and positive images of what will happen. This is partially effective, but it often creates an inner conflict.

In the Power Talk System we get right to the root of the problem. We don't start with the branches, or even the trunk. *It's only by destroying the roots of our fear that we can really be ourselves.*

How 'complexes' are formed − and ways to get rid of them

All fear arises between the announcement of an event and our association of it with past events. This is what psychologists call a 'complex', because it entails numerous cerebral associations all arising at the same time.

Here is an example:

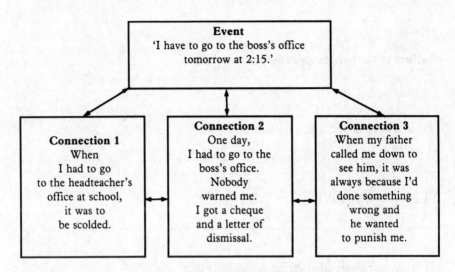

These are examples of associations which lead to a complex.

Study this example. What does it tell you? First of all, you will notice that all the connections are *negative*, and are associated with fear.

How to discover your Negative References

Think for a minute: are there more *positive* or *negative* images in your brain? Which ones are most often activated when you have to speak in public?

Now make a list of negative images (or Negative References) which you associate with the idea of speaking in public:

Speaking in public is like

_____

Being alone in front of a group is like

_____

Talking to strangers is like

_____

Being the focus of a meeting is like

_____

Feeling other people looking at me is like

_____

Being under observation by others is like

_____

Risking rejection is like

_____

Talking to people of the opposite sex is like

_____

Being criticised is like

_____

Expressing myself in front of superiors or authority figures is like

_____

Risking failure in front of others is like

_____

Did you answer all the questions? No? Well, work through them again, and *seriously* this time. How do you expect to make progress if you refuse to participate? You now have the opportunity – probably for the first time in your life – to clear up the problems which have been hindering you since childhood.

By reading this book, you have decided to put an end, once and for all, to your problems of expression and communication. DON'T PUT IT OFF FOR LATER! Get back to the questions, take the time to answer them completely and then write down all the scenes, thoughts and negative impressions associated with speaking in public that you can think of.

This book belongs to you. No one will be standing behind you, looking over your shoulder at what you write. It's like your own secret PTS journal. So don't be afraid to confide your most intimate thoughts.

It's by being perfectly sincere and honest with yourself that you will make progress.

All right? Have you got everything down on paper? Then let's continue.

How to de-activate your stage-fright

You might have heard this anecdote, concerning the great actress Sarah Bernhardt. One day she asked a young actress whether or not she suffered from stage-fright when she had to appear on stage. 'Oh no, Madame,' the young actress replied. 'Well,' Sarah Bernhardt said, 'don't worry, it will come, along with talent!'

There are a number of such ideas associated with stage-fright which are inherent in our way of thinking: 'You can never get rid of stage-fright.' 'You can control stage-fright, but you can't conquer it.' 'Stage-fright is necessary for performing well in public.'

Nothing is further from the truth.

I (Christian) had to deal with accepted falsehoods, concerning money, when I started out in business. 'You have to work hard to make a living.' 'You get nothing for nothing' etc. That's why I found myself working 15 hours a day. If I didn't, I felt guilty. There's always a Judeo-Christian ethic trying to put ready-made ideas into our minds. After getting rid of all these false truths, I realised that you can make a lot more money by working very little, and that you don't have to suffer to succeed.

The same goes for stage-fright. We think it's the price you have to pay to perform well. It's a little like the curse placed on Adam and Eve after their expulsion from Paradise: 'You will bear in suffering.' Giving a speech is like giving birth. And just as there are methods to give birth *without pain*, so the Power Talk System allows you to avoid, in most cases, the pain of stage-fright.

And don't think you'll be missing anything! On the contrary, all the energy that you're used to expending to control your stage-fright, those senseless efforts you make to hide your fears and control yourself, can be directed into your speech. You will be completely in tune with your audience, antennae extended, ready to give the best of yourself.

All the Negative References you noted on your list can be de-activated.

Think of your brain as a large garden. You usually follow the same path when you walk in it. It's smoothed out, your traces are there. Then one day you decide to take another path, to see other parts of your inner garden. If you continue taking this new path, the old one will gradually disappear, and the grass and bushes will cover it over. In other words, you have to create new cerebral paths in your mind.

One of the first things the Power Talk System does is to teach you how to create an Active Positive Reference Reserve so that you can link new (and potentially frightening) situations to positive memories.

How to create your Active Positive Reference Reserve

These are the steps you must take in order to create your Active Positive Reference Reserve (A.P.R.R.):

1. Choose communication situations where you had to address a group. If you don't have any, take situations where you were talking to just one person.

2. Choose situations where you felt *good*, in body as well as mind.

3. Take situations where you were *enthusiastic*, as if propelled by some inner fire, so that nothing could stand in your way. You will be speaking, in these cases, about something you know well and cherish.

4. Choose events that *ended well*, which means they brought you recognition and rewards (applause, smiles, congratulations, gestures of tenderness or affection etc.)

5. Recall every detail of these scenes: colours, movements, sounds, impressions and sensations, tastes, textures – the more *details* the better.

6. Describe at least three of these situations:

_____

_____

_____

In the days to come, get into the habit of recalling these scenes at least five times a day, and reliving them mentally.

If you have the opportunity to relax before doing this, all the better. But even if you have to do it while you're busy with something else, the important thing is to fill your field of consciousness with these scenes, and thus enrich your A.P.R.R. (Active Positive Reference Reserve), either by improving your images or by finding new ones.

The more you activate these images, the more force they will have, and the more your negative complexes with be replaced by positive complexes which will lead you to the road of success.

Define your Reference Guide

Now that you have a collection of positive references, you will be able to put together a key image – a composite – which will serve as a reference in most situations which call for oral expression.

Our subconscious does not differentiate between *memory, reality*, and things that are only *intensely imagined*.

Here, as an example, is a Reference Guide (R.G.) from one of our students:

'It takes place at my home, on my birthday. I have no warning, and when I get home and Gail opens the door, I can feel her joy. I feel a current of love passing through my entire being. I cross the hallway to the living-room. The lights go on and – surprise! All my friends are there. My dearest friends. There are gifts piled up on a table. They sing 'Happy Birthday' and applaud. I shake their hands, hug all my friends and walk over to the little platform with Gail's piano. Everyone is silent. I feel good, safe and secure, surrounded by friends. My heart overflows with thanks. And so, in very simple terms, I explain how touched I am by their attention, I tell them I appreciate it, and thank them. Everyone laughs. Filled with emotion, I wish them all a wonderful evening. More applause. Gail and my son Peter are beside me. I take them both in my arms, I feel fine, happy to be with the ones I love, happy to have expressed my friendship and love. A gentle warmth bathes my body with a feeling of happiness and well-being.'

Here's another example, this time Stephanie's R.G.:

'I am invited to a dinner party. Everyone there seems to be someone important: intellectuals, writers, a couple of university professors, a few performers. The person who greets me is a close friend, and I'm very happy to see her again. She introduces me, and mentions my profession. Somebody asks me a question. I answer, relaxed, passionate on the subject of my work. There's silence all round. Everyone listens to me attentively. I feel a current flowing between my audience and myself. For the rest of the evening, I'm the centre of attention, and the conversation is all about the subject I brought up. I'm happy because I'd always thought I had nothing to say in situations like this. I feel this inner victory like a series of waves of joy that flow over me, submerging me. The next day my friend calls and tells me I was a perfect stimulus for the evening, that she'd been afraid of this dinner, but that thanks to me it was a complete success. She confides that a number of guests found me beautiful and brilliant, and that she hopes I can come to the next party.'

Now it's your turn. You can use a real event, but feel free to add as many positive elements as you can. Describe your Reference Guide (R.G.) in as much detail as possible:

_____

_____

_____

Did you remember to enrich your R.G. with sensations of smell, taste, sight, sound, as well as internal thoughts?

How to transform negative into positive

It's said that 'Problems are opportunities in working clothes.' In other words, all difficulties, all failures, contain *positive elements*. It's often from the period of learning that we gain the most satisfaction.

Say, for example, you're supposed to speak after one of your colleagues, and he or she doesn't arrive. Surprise! You stammer and stutter and don't know what to do. Your colleague arrives just at that moment and just manages to get you off the hook.

One way to interpret the situation would be to say, 'I'm really no good. The slightest thing throws me off balance.' Another way would be to say, 'This is a good lesson. Next time, I'll be prepared for such an eventuality.

All I have to do is start my speech as if nothing had happened, and give more time to the question and answer period than was planned. No one will notice a thing.'

Now go back to pages 27 and 28, and one by one transform each of these Negative References into something positive.

- One way to do this is to *put yourself in the place of the person (or persons) you were speaking to.* If you'd been them, what *positive thoughts* could you have had concerning the person who was the centre of attention (you)?
- Change your point of view. Look at the situation through the eyes of others rather than your own for a change.
- Think about what you *could have done* to make things turn out differently.
- One of the most advanced techniques for transforming these kinds of situations into positive references is to connect them with a positive image. It's a long exercise, which usually takes several minutes for each association. You take your R.G. and fuse it with the past Negative Reference, until you're left with only one image. Try it, if only once. The effects are astonishing. This technique 'de-activates' Negative References.

Take all the time you need to work on your Negative References. If you have a lot of them it might take more than a week. But it's indispensable to be able to play freely with your references, and to learn how to make them positive.

How others perceive you

It's very difficult to accept the fact that people do not perceive us *as we are*, but modify their vision and all other sense perceptions according to their prejudices and priorities. (It's even more difficult to accept that we do this about ourselves!)

A classic example consists of looking at the drawing shown over the page.

If you expect to see a pretty young woman that's generally what you'll see.

If, on the other hand, you're prepared to see an old hag, then that's what you'll see.

Both women are in the same portrait, but *our perception of things dictates how we see them* and blocks one or the other interpretation.

Try shifting your image from the young woman to the old, and vice versa.

In the same way that it's indispensable to learn to see the positive in every situation, you should be able to change your point of view at will. It's precisely this 'suppleness of mind' that will make you a good communicator.

What we've just experienced can be explained by the following diagram:

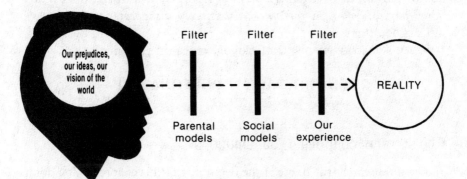

As this diagram shows, people have a distorted vision of the world. This doesn't mean that they're wrong, or that they're lying about what they see. No. Another drawing explains how different points of view arise:

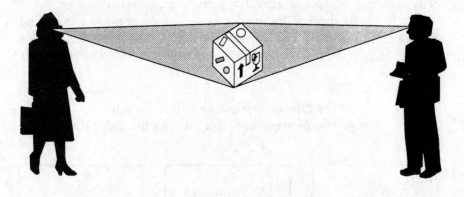

As long as you cannot change places with another − or others − and perceive things *from their point of view* you will have problems communicating.

Other people are not prosecutors or judges

Very often we think that other people see us objectively, that they scrutinise us, and can see us in all our 'nakedness', right through our defences. Not at all. They are lost in their own filters, thoughts, problems.

What they report is never an objective account of what you do, but a distorted reflection.

In other words, other people are not prosecutors or judges. They are always *partial*, their vision is always distorted by their own filters, and *a large part of your fear of others will simply disappear* once you have understood this.

When somebody seems to attack you, repeat in your mind:

'I DON'T TAKE IT PERSONALLY!'

The secret of controlling your emotions

Do you remember the quote at the beginning of this chapter? 'You don't run away because you're afraid. You're afraid because you run away from your fear.' Its author, William James (1842–1910), also said, 'One of the greatest discoveries of my generation is that you can change your life by changing your state of mind.'

In the preceding pages, we've seen how important it is to 'change your state of mind' in order to get rid of complexes, especially in relation to others. But in the work of William James we find the origin of a recent and fundamental discovery that forces us to reconsider everything we've always thought about stage-fright and oral expression in general. Here is that discovery:

Every emotion originates in a thought.
Change the thought and you change the emotion.

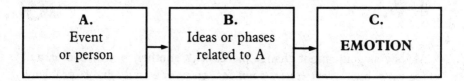

This means that, when William James says that we are afraid (emotion) because we run away from fear, *the origin of this flight is a thought.*

We will see, in another chapter, how to modify our thoughts in order to avoid stage-fright, or to create a desired emotion. Meanwhile, each time you experience an emotion, try to find *what you said to yourself immediately before that feeling.* It's a difficult exercise, but extremely useful. Do this for positive emotions such as joy, enthusiasm and love, as well as for negative emotions like sadness, fear, discouragement or anger.

You should become aware of the difference between the *events* that spark emotions and what you tell yourself when they occur. You will realise that it's not the events themselves that affect you, but your personal filters through which you see them and the inner dialogue that they trigger off.

And continue to re-activate your A.P.R.R. numerous times a day.

In the next chapter we will look at some general principles to make your communication more effective, but, before reading this, answer the following questions to find out how much you now know about how to overcome stage-fright and build your confidence.

QUIZ

1. Tick the appropriate box:
   Fear is:
   ☐ **A** A useless negative association.
   ☐ **B** A preparation for action.
   ☐ **C** A necessary evil.

2. Complete the following sentence: 'All the energy that you usually expend in controlling your stage-fright, all your senseless efforts to master your emotions and hide your nervousness, all that energy could be better invested in

   _____.'

3. Our subconscious ☐ does ☐ does not differentiate between memories of reality and what is only intensely imagined or dreamed.

4. One of the reasons that it's hard for us to see the positive side of certain events is:
   ☐ **A** Because our perceptions are blocked, and allow us to see things from only one point of view.
   ☐ **B** Because most people do not react to us in a positive way.
   ☐ **C** Because being positive results in dropping your defences and not being careful.

5. When someone attacks you, it's because:
   ☐ **A** He (or she) dislikes you personally.
   ☐ **B** He has found out who you really are, because you weren't able to hide yourself well enough.
   ☐ **C** He is a victim of his own limited perception of reality, and needs to be helped.

Answers
1. B.
2. Your speech or presentation.
3. Does not.
4. A.
5. C.

CHAPTER 3

HOW TO COMMUNICATE BETTER

'The old idea which holds that words possess some kind of magic power is false: but it is the distortion of an important truth. Words do have a magic power – but not in the way magicians thought, and not on the objects that they tried to manipulate. The magic of words lies in the influence they have on the brains of those who use them.'

ALDOUS HUXLEY

The 3 essential rules for effective communication

Did you know that there are communications upon which thousands of lives depend?

At this very moment, while you read these lines, thousands of people risk death if these communications fail. Your own life, I'm sure, has been in the hands of these communicators more than once, without your being aware of it.

What do we mean? Airline pilots are an obvious example. All those lives depend on the dialogue between pilots and air-control towers. If there is a misunderstanding, navigational errors can result and accidents can happen.

So how do pilots and air-traffic controllers make sure that their communications are precise and efficient? We can surely learn a few things from the techniques that they use.

1. They speak the same language: English.

This isn't as obvious as it might seem. I've been to dozens of conferences where the speaker didn't speak the same language as the audience.

How is this possible? Well, each specialised field has a kind of unique language which others often don't understand. If you are not involved in economics, do you understand that:

> 'From the purely methodological standpoint, it is doubtful whether any antithesis is falser than that which has sometimes been set up as between an emphasis on the importance of a study of economic institutions and their functioning, on the one hand, upon that type of calculation by "economising" individuals, which represents the subject matter of the core of "traditional" economic analysis.'

That was written a few years ago. Don't think for a moment that things are any different today. The techniques and vocabulary of confusing communication have made a lot of progress since then.

And don't think that every word in the dictionary is familiar to your audience, even if they speak the same language as you: the average person is said to have a vocabulary of about 2000 words, while the dictionary contains about 75,000!

The solution? *Put yourself in other people's shoes.* Consider what you say in the light of their likely powers of comprehension, and make sure that any complicated words or technical data are clearly explained.

Robert Barrat, a great reporter and editor-in-chief of the magazine *Paris-Match* for seven years explained:

> 'When I write an article or give a conference, I imagine myself speaking to a teenager, about 15 or 16 years old, like my son Patrick.'

Conclusion: if you want to speak the same language as your listeners, use simple vocabulary that can be understood by all.

2. They make sure that every word is heard clearly.

There are factors which can limit communication. *Intensity* for example. If you don't speak loudly enough, people will have to make more of an effort to pay attention, and you will not be able to *hold their attention* for very long.

Then there's noise. In radio communication, noise is caused by interference. In an auditorium it is caused by external noise – coughing, chairs moving, whispering – as well as the 'interior noise' of your listeners.

The most difficult thing is to break through the barrier of your listeners' preoccupations. People are constantly preoccupied by thousands of things. They think about their own problems and are not available to listen to yours. If you don't find a way to capture their attention immediately, their immediately, their 'interior noise' will prevent them from hearing what you have to say.

The same goes for you. If you're not *completely concentrated* on what you're saying, you risk losing the thread of your ideas because of your own 'interior noise'.

Conclusion: insist on silence in the auditorium or conference room (do not begin or continue until there is complete silence) and capture your listeners' attention right from the start. (We'll see how later on.)

3. They repeat important information

Obviously this is the best way to *make sure* that you are understood.

It's not always easy to get 'feedback' from an audience, to allow you to verify if what you said has been understood. There are, however, ways to promote audience participation, which we'll look at later on.

If you can't get people to repeat the information you wish to communicate, then do the next best thing and *repeat it yourself*, in different words, to make sure it has sunk in.

As Napoleon said 'Repetition is the best rhetoric.'

Repetition can help you to make your point clear and gives emphasis. An American senator attending the United Nations was tired of a vote always being postponed:

'A vote must be taken now, immediately. Immediately, not tomorrow. Immediately, not after more speeches from the chair. Immediately, not after Mr Manuilsky gets some more advice from his advisers. Immediately.'

The vote was taken right away.

How better to understand the psychology of those around you

In 1947, two psychologists, Allport and Postman, conducted the following experiment: they showed people a photograph of a well-dressed black person being attacked in a subway by a poorly dressed white person holding a razor.

Invariably, people who were shown the image for a few seconds, and then asked to describe what they saw, reported a *white person* being attacked by a *black*!

We conducted this experiment ourselves several times, during our seminars on oral expression. The picture was shown to one person, who then described it to his or her neighbour, who described it to the next person, and so on.

Once, the mother of one of us attended one of these seminars and, to our great surprise, she turned out to be the one who 'transformed' the white aggressor into a black, despite the fact that she has many black friends and is opposed to any form of racism.

This experiment illustrates once more the power of our mental filters.

But here we go *one step further*: not only do people select those elements of reality which interest them – and only those elements – they also *see things in events which are not there at all*!

Therefore if you communicate something new to people, they must associate it with something they already know in order to be able to understand it. If what you say contradicts their previous beliefs, they will forget it, or won't even hear it. The way to get round this is to use images or comparisons which relate to already existing cerebral patterns.

A golf teacher, trying to improve someone's swing, might say, 'Ring the bell! Ring the bell'. Even if you don't play golf, you can imagine that the image of hitting a large bell with a stick would be easier to comprehend than a detailed technical description of each movement of the body necessary to perform a golf swing correctly. It's by using *familiar images* that we can successfully modify the brain patterns of others. And not only can images be evoked through sentences, but words themselves are often image-provoking.

Which words work and why?

Certain words evoke more powerful images than others. And one fascinating thing about listening to great speakers is to note just how much attention they devote to words that evoke images rather than concepts.

Exercise

Underline the image words and phrases in the following text:

I entered the first empty compartment I found, unaware that an invisible travelling companion was already there. Our fascinating conversation would keep me awake for the rest of the night.

The train rocked gently. I watched the lights of Stockholm fade little by little, then got under the covers and waited for sleep to come. But then, on the bench opposite my bed I saw a book, forgotten by a passenger.

I picked it up mechanically and read over the first few lines: five minutes later, I was still reading, avidly, as if a friend were telling me where to find a treasure.

The treasure was my memory. I learned that everyone possesses an amazing memory, with fantastic capabilities, but that those who know how to use this marvellous faculty are few and far between. The book explained how even the least gifted person could, after only one concentrated reading, easily remember information as complicated as a list of the 100 largest cities in the world, as well as their respective populations!

It seemed impossible that my own dull, 40-year-old brain could ever retain lists of numbers, dates, cities and names. I had been a terrible history student . . . recalling dates and places were the bane of my school days, even when my brain was fresh and young. I decided to test the book's theories and see whether or not they were true.

Answer

Enter – empty compartment – invisible companion – morning – fascinating – the train rocked gently – lights fading little by little – got under the covers – waited for sleep – noticed a book – bench opposite my bed – traveller – I picked it up mechanically – I read avidly – treasure – my own dull 40-year-old brain – school – fresh young memory.

Now compare that passage with this newspaper article:

Charged with resolving once and for all the conflict that has existed between government and immigrant workers for the last 25 years, Senator Raymond has recommended economic measures that are hardly in keeping with the President's policy of restraint, which was made very clear in the Presidential elections held in 1981.

His programme of total amnesty, with no penalties for tax evasion practised by these workers over the last 25 years, as well as interest-free loans to help indebted rural workers and their families who have migrated to urban centres establish themselves, improved unemployment and retirement benefits, workman's compensation and another programme to compensate war veterans, is totally inconsistent with the tone of spending restraint called for by the President.

Mr Raymond is proposing nothing short of an exclusive social welfare programme, available only to a limited community. Local mayors have stated that they are opposed to such a programme and will petition the government. They claim the money should be available to the community at large. They claim they have already established repatriation offices in their sectors, and are handling the problem well.

It can only be concluded that Senator Raymond, in his sweeping generosity, is gambling on the support of visible minority groups in his bid for appointment to the post of Secretary of State. Minority group leaders, meanwhile, have decided to wait and see . . .

What are the image words and phrases in this text?

Answer
Conflict − penalties − war − gambling.

The key to make your conversations more interesting

Which text was easier to read? The first one, of course. As the French essayist Alain said, 'An abstract style is bad. Your sentences should be full of chairs, tables, rocks, men and women.'

Here's a diagram, illustrating the principle of imagery:

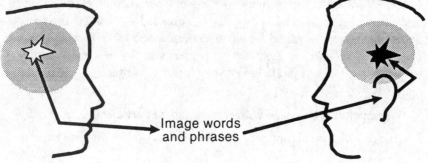

Image words
and phrases

But that's not all. At the moment, we're talking about images that are *consciously perceived*. There are countless other messages which can be communicated on a *subconscious* level. We'll be discussing that in the next chapter. First complete the following quiz and see how well you have understood the topics we have just discussed.

QUIZ

1. The average person has a vocabulary of:
- ☐ **A** 3500 words.
- ☐ **B** 600 words.
- ☐ **C** 2000 words.

2. How can you prevent your listeners' 'inner noise' from interfering with your presentation?
- ☐ **A** Talk faster.
- ☐ **B** Talk louder.
- ☐ **C** Capture their attention from the start.

3. How can you easily modify the brain patterns of others?
- ☐ **A** Through images.
- ☐ **B** Through conceptual words.
- ☐ **C** Through gesture.

4. What is the most powerful form of rhetoric?
- ☐ **A** Kindness.
- ☐ **B** Repetition.
- ☐ **C** Salesmanship.

Answers
1. C.
2. C.
3. A.
4. B.

CHAPTER 4

MASTER THE SECRETS OF BODY LANGUAGE

'Who you are speaks so loudly that I can't hear what you're saying.'
RALPH WALDO EMERSON

Let me tell you of the occasion when I (Christian) became aware of the connection between body language and persuasion. At the time I was an assistant manager for a publishing firm, still new on the job. On this particular morning I was going to have the chance to work with Paul Costa, top salesman with the company for the previous three years.

Paul Costa sells encyclopaedias. Lots of encyclopaedias. At that time he was selling *twice as many* as the next best salesman in the company. And he does it door to door, which is the hardest way to sell.

What's his secret?

He is a large man, with the look of a teddy bear. A deep voice, calm and reassuring.

I watched as he made his first sale of the day. What I noticed right away was his body language, and his extraordinary sense of observation. As soon as the client showed the least sign of interest, he would jump in with a conclusive question. And when he was winding up to his final pitch, he was nodding his head 'yes' in such a reassuring way that the offer became exciting and irresistible.

Actually, there were many reasons why he was so successful: he had a notebook in which he kept track of all the objections he has had to deal with, and the best responses to them; immediate withdrawal as soon as he felt he was wasting his time with a client who liked to talk but not buy; short sentences rich with images. But the most amazing thing was the way he would observe his listeners, and all the suggestions he made using only his body.

65% of your messages are expressed by your body

Since that day, I have become very interested in the power of persuasion through body language. According to studies conducted at Stanford University:

● 45 per cent of a message is expressed by the body,
● 20 per cent by the tone of voice,
● 35 per cent by the words (and phrases) you use.

The Canadian communications theorist Marshall MacLuhan came up with the now famous statement: 'THE MEDIUM IS THE MESSAGE.' This means that the way in which a message is transmitted is as important as the message itself.

Maybe you think that you can rely solely on words to get your message across? Maybe you think all you have to do to get others interested in what you say, and to make yourself understood, is to choose the right words and put them together into pretty phrases?

This might be partially true for written messages. But it's completely false as far as the spoken word goes. Because in spoken language, communication does not take place on the word level alone. Sixty-five per cent of spoken communication has nothing to do with words, and depends on things like:

● the voice itself,
● breathing,
● looking,
● gestures,
● movement,
● dress.

In fact, your own body is a veritable orchestra!

If you want to excel in the art of oral communication, you must first *learn to direct* that orchestra.

Now, what are your instruments?

5 secrets for a pleasant and powerful voice

Have you seen *Singing In The Rain*, the musical comedy starring Gene Kelly? The action takes place in the era of silent films. A young, silent-screen actress is adored by millions of fans, until her first talking picture, when they discover she has a voice like a tin can. And so the goddess falls from her pedestal!

Aside from Douglas Fairbanks and Charlie Chaplin, very few of the silent stars were able to make the transition to talking pictures. And this illustrates just how important the voice is for social success, in the cinema and as in every other walk of life as well.

But there's one important point that hasn't been mentioned yet: the human voice is a very malleable instrument. Which means that there are *practically no limits to its perfectibility*.

Did you know, for example, that Winston Churchill had a horrible stutter when he started his career? And yet, through will-power and practice, he became one of the most brilliant orators of the twentieth century.

Having an accent, or a slight speech impediment – on condition that you can be understood, and that it doesn't constantly distract your audience – can be an *asset*. Audiences appreciate the effort it takes for someone to speak in a language other than his or her own. They will often even help out with a missing word or expression. The 'complicity' thus established between speaker and audience is a factor that shouldn't be overlooked.

How to place your voice

Actors who give courses on oral expression tend to worry too much about the voice. Of course it's important. But, aside from a few simple voice techniques which we'll look at together, the really important thing for an orator is *comfort*. If your voice is not placed correctly, it will get tired, and in an hour you won't have any voice left.

The most important thing to know is that the pitch of your voice is a question of *habit*. Like all other habits, this one can be modified. Of course it takes time, but there are also numerous benefits:

● less fatigue when speaking in public,
● added charm,
● a larger register (for greater interest),
● a closer relationship between your voice and your personality – your voice will 'ring true'.

Exercise
Start by breathing in deeply. Then empty your lungs while saying 'AAAAH ...' At first, use a relatively high pitch, then gradually bring it down. Pay attention to *the vibrations* resonating in your jaw, your skull,

your rib-cage. Note the moment when these vibrations are strongest. You'll also notice how your voice can relax you, like an internal massage. Start again until you find your optimum pitch (the point at which the vibrations are strongest). Do the exercise with each of the vowels: A E I O U, and finish with 'MMMMMH ...' Compare your optimum pitch with your habitual voice level. Then try to adjust your usual voice level accordingly.

Articulate correctly

Most people have no trouble pronouncing the vowels correctly. But articulating consonants is another story.

Actually, *articulation* is more difficult to teach people than *pronunciation*. Most young infants will learn to pronounce most vowels spontaneously.

To become aware of your articulation, there is only *one indispensable method*: tape yourself and listen to your voice.

You may say that a recording has nothing to do with the quality of your 'real' voice. Your 'real' voice is much deeper, fuller, better sounding. Why? Because what you're hearing as your 'real' voice is really a blend of what other people hear *and* the *vibrations of your voice, which reach your ear internally, but which others do not hear*. It's like putting your ear right up against a drum: the sound is not the same as it is from a distance.

Your 'real' voice − the one your listeners hear − is the one on the tape. And that's the one you have to work on.

How?

For the simplest exercise you need a pencil, a quiet place and a little time.

1. Start by talking with the pencil held so it points straight out from between your teeth. This works your labial muscles.

2. Next put the pencil horizontally in your mouth, well back, like a horse's bit, and continue talking. This is recommended as a warm-up for your mouth muscles, before delivering a speech.

Voice rhythm

There's nothing more sleep-inducing than a monotonal voice. It's the variations in tone that liven up a voice. Many professors, lecturers, conference leaders etc. are neither heard nor understood for the simple reason that they don't vary their tonality.

Of course, everyone varies tonality instinctively to some extent in normal, everyday conversation. If we were sitting face to face in my office, having a discussion about something or other, you would surely use inflections in your voice which you wouldn't even be aware of.

But talking in front of an audience, or a group of people, is a totally different ballgame. And in those kinds of circumstances, it is important to exercise conscious control of your intonation. It plays a decisive role in the *impact* your words will have on other people.

Rhythm depends on three factors: intensity, intonation and speed.

1. Intensity

As you read through this book, you will see that certain passages are italicised, others are indented, others are in capitals or centred. This kind of presentation prevents the eyes from getting tired of looking at the text, by offering visual variations.

The same goes for speeches. Underlined words and phrases are spoken more loudly. Centred passages might be spoken more softly, in a more intimate tone.

In short, you can emphasise certain passages in your text by changing the *intensity* of your voice.

Let's set up a code: (▶) means you speak loudly; (▶▶) means very loudly; (▲) means normal voice and (▼) means softly.

Now read the following text and add the symbols which you think would best indicate the appropriate intensity:

( ) How did the President of United States and his party find the 150,000,000 dollars they needed for his electoral campaign?
Simply with the aid of letters addressed to the electors. ( ) And you can do the same. ( ) Whether you're a businessman, a politician, a

storekeeper, or a young entrepreneur, you can by writing ( )
attractive, ( ) convincing, ( ) powerful letters ( ) achieve the
success you are striving for ten times as fast.
( ) It isn't a question of some ( ) special gift: ( ) the techniques can
be learned, and are available to everyone.
( ) It isn't a question of ( ) money: ( ) most people who have
achieved success in this field had no capital to speak of when they
started. Paper and a typewriter were all they needed.
It isn't a question of ( ) time: ( ) writing a letter doesn't take more
than an hour or two, and can result in millions of dollars in returns.
( ) So what do you need to succeed?
( ) You need to know the 'tricks of the trade.' ( ) Until now, the
techniques of Direct Marketing were available only to the initiated
few. But now, these techniques have been revealed for everyone to
discover, in this course: ( ) 'How To Write Letters That ( ) Sell'.

Solution

(▲) How did the President of United States and his party find the
150,000,000 dollars they needed for his electoral campaign?
Simply with the aid of letters addressed to the electors. (▶) And you
can do the same. (▲) Whether you're a businessman, a politician, a
storekeeper, or a young entrepreneur, you can, by writing (▶)
attractive, (▶▶) convincing, (▶▶) powerful letters (▶) achieve the
success you are striving for ten times as fast.
(▼) It isn't a question of some (▲) special gift: (▼) the techniques
can be learned, and are available to everyone.
(▼) It isn't a question of (▲) money: (▼) most people who have
achieved success in this field had no capital to speak of when they
started. Paper and a typewriter were all they needed.
It isn't a question of (▲) time: (▼) writing a letter doesn't take more
than an hour or two, and can result in millions of dollars in returns.
(▶) So what do you need to succeed?
(▶▶) You need to know the 'tricks of the trade'. (▲) Until now, the
techniques of Direct Marketing were available only to the initiated
few. But now, these techniques have been revealed for everyone to
discover, in this course: (▶) 'How To Write Letters That (▶▶) Sell'.

Of course, this is only our opinion of what could be done. The intensity
could also be varied in other ways and still work perfectly well. What
should be remembered is that a monotonous sound, without changes in
intensity, will put an audience to sleep.

2. Intonation – the 30/10 Power Formula

Intonation is what adds 'life' to your voice. To exercise your voice and improve your intonation – its rise and fall – nothing is better than *reading out loud*. There are other benefits too. Millard Bennet, one of the greatest salesmen in America, introduced me to this technique. He calls it the '30/10 Power Formula'.

'Suppose', he says, 'it were possible to spend 30 minutes a day, for the next 12 months, with the greatest thinkers the world has produced – past or present.' Think about the effect that would have. Would it improve your self-confidence? Wouldn't you be more relaxed in front of an audience? The answer is yes.

How to do it? Here's Millard Bennet's secret:

There's a difficult and an easy way to accomplish almost anything. Over the year, I've tried numerous methods to acquire knowledge. Finally, after years of trial and error, I found a very simple method: I passed it on to others, and the results they obtained with the method were so extraordinary that I gave it a name the '30/10 Power Formula'. All it requires is 30 minutes a day – 10 minutes reading out loud and 20 minutes of in-depth study of a passage, whether it be literature or listening to educational and/or motivational cassettes.

'Thirty minutes a day spent in this way will certainly increase your knowledge, and assure your growing success in whatever area you desire. But few people have the ambition to adopt such a program, and fewer still the will-power to see it through. But if you do it, you will make steady progress each day, so that there will soon be very little difference between your dreams and your reality.'

Not only will this formula help improve your intonation, it will also enrich your vocabulary and your knowledge. For example, you could read this book out loud, for 10 minutes a day. Many books on personal development are perfectly suited to the 30/10 formula.

3. Speed

Voice speed means the number of words spoken per minute.

In December 1961, President John F. Kennedy gave a speech at the rate of 327 words per minute!

His record was broken by a British sports reporter, Raymond Glendenning, who managed 176 words in 30 seconds, while giving the commentary on a greyhound race!

But there's no mention in the history books of how many Americans actually understood Kennedy's speech.

The best advice I can give you is the following:

**Put yourself in your listener's place:
choose a speed that will be understood by all.**

Use all the will-power you have. We know it's not always easy to control your speed. Often we speak quickly because we 'can't wait' to finish, because the tension resulting from stage-fright makes us go faster, or because what we're saying seems so obvious to us that we forget that others are hearing it for the first time.

Remember that there is a gap between 'transmission' and 'reception' of messages.

Once you have mastered this first point, you can apply a second principle:

Learn to vary your speed according to the text.

This will add more life to your words, and will help your listeners follow what you're saying. A slower speed will let them know that a passage is more important, and should be retained. A faster speed will inform them that a passage is expository or descriptive and need not be retained. A fast pace followed by a sudden long pause will create suspense etc.

Of course, if you slow the pace down too much, you risk putting your audience to sleep.

Variations in speed could be charted as follows:

Accelerate   →
Decelerate   ←
Normal speed   ▶
Brief pause   □
Long pause   ■

Read out loud the following passage taken from *The Creature of the Sea*, a novel by Alfred Van Vogt. Try to vary your speed, making the text more alive and captivating. Note your speed variations in the spaces provided:

( ) My god, what are you doing? ( ) This place is full of sharks. ( ) For god's sake, say something, stop looking at me like that . . . those horrible eyes . . . ( ) I . . . ( ).
( ) He dropped the empty gun and grabbed a harpoon. ( ) But with a shout the creature was on him, and with terrible strength picked him up and threw him overboard. ( ) The water boiled as long,

cigar-like shapes rose from the depths to the surface. ( ) Soon the turquoise water was stained with blood, and the creature picked up the oars and started rowing.

Here's the same passage, as I imagine it should be read out loud:

(→) My god, what are you doing? (▶) This place is full of sharks. (→) For god's sake, say something, stop looking at me like that ... those horrible eyes ... (□) I ... (■).
(→) He dropped the empty gun and grabbed a harpoon. (▶) But with a shout the creature was on him, and with terrible strength picked him up and threw him overboard. (▶) The water boiled as long, cigar-like shapes rose from the depths to the surface. (←) Soon the turquoise water was stained with blood, and the creature picked up the oars and started rowing.

This exercise gives you a taste of the effects that can be created by varying voice speed. As you can see, it sometimes doesn't take much to add impact to our words!

How to increase the power of your facial expressions

'Eyes are the windows of the soul ...' wrote Pascal.

Open any novel and you'll find a wealth of adjectives describing the characters' eyes: inquisitive, friendly, tender, suspicious, confident, inscrutable, curious, astonished, indifferent, ironic, suggestive, etc.

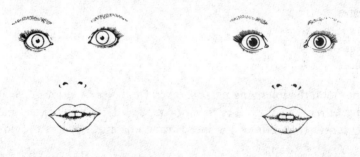

Look at these two women's faces. Which is more appealing? Ninety-five per cent of people will say the one on the right. Why?

Your Answer: _____

Our Answer: Because in the face on the right the pupils are dilated.

When you experience emotion, your pupils dilate. When you pretend to experience emotion, they remain closed.

**The subconscious is very sensitive
to dilation of the pupils.**

Even at a considerable distance the result is the same. When two identical photographs, of which one has been retouched to enlarge the pupils, are presented to a group, the one with the dilated pupils will always be preferred.

So your eyes are expressive in this way. But that's not all.

When you think, according to Neuro-Linguistic Programming, your inner experience is expressed by your eye movements. N.L.P. is a new behavioural science designed by John Grinder and Richard Bandler, resulting from the study of great psychotherapists like Virginia Satir, Frederick Perls and Milton Erickson. The relationship between thought process and eye movement is as follows:

1. Fabricated Visual Images
When you imagine a project, a scene, a face . . . in the future (up, right).

2. Fabricated spoken sounds and spoken words
When you say something, or create a sound (right).

3. Remembered visual images
When you look for an image in your memory (up, left).

4. Remembered sounds and spoken words
When you recall a sound, a word, music etc (left).

5. Sensations, feelings, inner perceptions
When you feel or sense something (down, right).

Experiment
Ask someone these questions, while observing their eye movements.

1. What would you look like if you let your beard grow?
   What if you had green hair?
   Imagine a flower that doesn't exist.
2. How would your name sound with a Russian accent?
   What music could turn your saucepan into a guitar?
3. What colour is your front door?
   Describe the form and colour of your mother's eyes.
4. What kind of music do you like to listen to?
   What does your father sound like when he calls you by your first name?
5. How do you feel when you sit in a rocking chair?
   How do you feel when you're in love?

You can also ask more complex questions, which will result in rapidly changing movements:

6. Imagine a toy car climbing up the side of the Eiffel Tower, blowing its horn . . .

Being aware of the relation between mental processes and eye movements is interesting to the effective communicator (whom you are becoming) for a number of reasons:

1. It shows that you can, while searching for a memory, allow your eyes to move in the corresponding direction. Your listeners will understand, and follow your train of thought. And what's more, these eye movements actually *make things easier*.
2. In small groups, or when talking to one person, you can learn a lot from eye movements.
3. By observing others, you can classify them as 'more visual', 'more auditive' or 'more emotional' according to their preference for various eye movements, and then *adapt your vocabulary to suit the way they think*. It's better to say 'You see . . .' or 'Look at it this way . . .' to visually oriented people. 'Listen to this . . .' to auditive people, and 'I feel that . . .' to emotionally oriented people!

How to control your audience with your eyes

We've seen how useful eyes are to express nuance. Eye movement is a language of its own, which most of us decode automatically.

But eye movements can also be an extraordinary method of controlling an audience. As long as your listeners are watching your eyes, they will remain attentive. So practise *sweeping the auditorium* with your eyes – either by staring at groups of three of four people at a time, each group seated in a different part of the room – or by not focusing your attention but sweeping the auditorium continuously.

The speaker's position is therefore very important. *Never allow anyone to sit in a dead space.*

Think about a magician: for the public to be taken in by a trick, the magician must absolutely be facing them straight on, so that he or she can't be observed from the side, from the dead spaces. The same goes for you.

Exercise
Turn off the sound while watching TV, and observe the way the characters use eye movements.

How to make your gestures free and natural

Let's recapitulate. We've seen that, aside from the words we use, the impact of what we say depends on a number of physical factors. Our eyes, the pitch of our voice, our intonation, the quality of articulation, variations in speed – all play an important role.

But our gestures also comprise a language. For example, crossed arms represent a position of defence, of turning inward. Keeping your hands in your pockets shows lack of respect for your audience, an 'I don't care' attitude.

An open hand symbolises peace (I have no weapon) and therefore expresses openness.

2 golden rules of a good body position

To communicate successfully:

1. *Plant yourself firmly on the ground.* Your posture expresses your stability – or your fragility. If you have to move around a lot in order not to lose your balance, you will express doubt and lack of self-confidence.

   On the other hand, if you adopt a position similar to judo, where the feet are spread to shoulder width, with your body-weight centred, you will express confidence and stability.

   Use the image of an oak firmly planted in the ground as a reference. (Of course this doesn't mean you shouldn't move at all!)

2. *Free your arms and hands.* Stage-fright will paralyse your gestures. They lose their scope. Instead of being extensions of your thoughts, your body becomes a rigid, inexpressive mass.

   The ideal thing would, of couse, be to study mime, or at least to play games like charades (maybe with your children) where you have to communicate without using your voice.

The closer the presentation date gets, the more your residual fears will grow. So what happens in your body?

The brain sends orders to the hypothalamus, which, with the help of stress hormones – 'stimulants' which provide temporary energy, like the caffeine in your coffee – prepares your body for action.

This process, which was very useful in prehistoric times when people had to defend themselves almost constantly against predators, has become less useful today.

But luckily the brain stays in control. What would happen if, in moments of intense stress (when you're very angry, for example) your brain didn't possess a *simultaneous inhibitory mechanism*? And what if this mechanism were not as strong as the energy created by the stress? You would attack people indiscriminately whenever you were angry, or turn on your heels and run every time you had to speak in public!

Do you remember the chart:

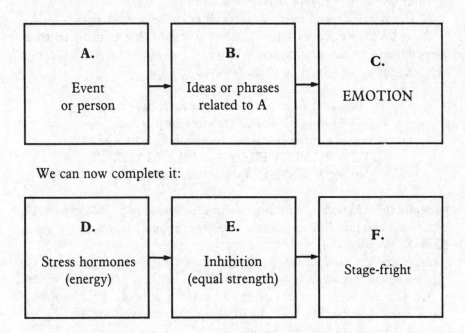

We can now complete it:

So, stress inhibits our behaviour, which results in paralysis, lack of memory, fast heart beats, etc – all symptoms of stage-fright.

Establish your space bubble

The preceding pages lead me to speak about a science that is still in its early stages of development: it's called the science of *proxemics*.

It studies the relations which are established between people, according to the relative positions which they occupy in space. It seeks to understand how and why certain positions can hinder communication, while others can be beneficial.

The American researcher E. T. Hall is one of the pioneers of the proxemic theory. He discovered that the acceptable distance between communicants varies from one culture to another, following well-established conventions.

For North Americans, for example, an 'intimate' distance between two people would be about 12 inches (30 cms); whereas in South America the distance is so minimal that the two faces almost touch. So if a South American meets a North American, the latter would have the tendency to back up in order to maintain an acceptable distance, while the former would always be trying to move closer. This is an example of the kinds of phenomenon that proxemics is interested in.

But proxemics doesn't only concern distance between people.

Actually, the nature of the relationship you establish with your audience depends on another very important factor: the way you move, and the way you use the space which has been reserved for you.

**The fact of using your space, of moving,
of being MOBILE, is very important
as far as communicating in public is concerned:
IT INDICATES THAT YOU HAVE TAKEN
POSSESSION OF YOUR SPACE.**

You can be a good communicator and still remain immobile in front of your microphone. But to become an efficient communicator, *you must learn to occupy your space.*

Miming a little scene, walking the length of the stage while scanning the audience, circling a blackboard – are all ways of occupying your space.

It's as if you were surrounded by an invisible bubble. When someone penetrates your bubble you feel ill at ease, unless you are seeking an intimate dialogue with that person.

Exercise

Ask a friend to stand about 15 yards from you and then advance slowly toward you. Concentrate on your bodily sensations. As soon as you feel a vibration, a reticence, a kind of violation of your territory, say STOP! Measure the distance. Do this a few times. This will give you an idea of the size of your personal bubble. In future, always try to have this space respected, to assure your well-being.

Animals and children are especially sensitive to the notion of 'territory'. The next time you meet a strange dog, for example, watch its reactions as you approach. Note how important your physical attitude is. If you're afraid, the dog will feel it and probably bark. If you're open and friendly, if you approach calmly without violating its territory, the dog will probably make friends with you.

The same goes for an audience. Your physical posture − looking like someone who is tired and submissive, or keeping your head raised to exude confidence and a winning attitude − can make all the difference. Remember:

> **Before starting to speak, remain silent, stand**
> **straight and solid on your feet, breathe**
> **calmly and cover the entire room with your**
> **eyes to take possession of your territory.**

The importance of clothing − professional tips

Have you noticed how much better you feel when you put your best suit on? If you look your best, you feel better. Why neglect this aspect of communication, which can become a definite asset? Take the time to bring out the best of your physical attributes.

Dress according to the circumstances. Sports clothes in a business meeting will make you uncomfortable. A very formal suit for a friendly meeting will make you appear stiff and stuffy.

Test your own degree of tolerance for differences in dress: the more different you feel, more or less, the more you will be noticed, and the more you expose yourself. Be aware, though, that an eccentric costume can also be a protective shield, like a mask. By attracting attention to the exterior aspect, it establishes a secret, interior space which can be comfortable to 'inhabit'. Uniforms − even the most gaudy − fulfil a similar function: a fragile person hides behind the mask of a character.

But most important is to feel comfortable:

- Choose comfortable clothes which permit easy breathing and freedom of movement. Get rid of everything that restricts you: collars, ties, belts, tight sleeves. They will enhance the feelings of paralysis, anxiety and suffocation which usually accompany stage-fright.
- Wear familiar 'lived-in' clothing, even if a brand new suit or dress might be more elegant. New outfits can result in unpleasant surprises like the professional lecturer I know who suffered from stage-fright only once, when he wore a pair of new shoes. He was used to walking up and down the stage while he spoke. But the soles of his new shoes were so slippery that he had to sit down, which changed his whole presentation and made him lose a lot of confidence.
- Dress lightly. Speaking in public − showing yourself − releases energy and therefore heat; stage-fright makes you hot; conference rooms and

auditoriums are often over-heated and underventilated, and the body heat of the audience will raise the temperature considerably.
● Choose colours you like, that you find reassuring.

Now, test yourself on your understanding of body language.

QUIZ

1. The words you use represent:
☐ **A**   Only 35 per cent of your message.
☐ **B**   45 per cent of your message.
☐ **C**   65 per cent of your message.

2. What happens to your eyes when you experience emotion?

3. Tick the statements you think are true:
☐ **A**   While delivering a speech, you should stare at one member of the audience and read the reactions of the rest of the audience through that person.
☐ **B**   Where members of your audience are seated is of no importance, as long as they can hear you.
☐ **C**   Establishing eye contact is important. It's like an invisible thread that binds you to your audience.
☐ **D**   Your gaze should sweep the room regularly, so that each person feels your control over them.

4. When you speak in public, you should always dress warmly.
☐ True ☐ False.

5. Like animals, humans have a space around them, a territory that you should respect.
☐ True ☐ False.

Answers
1. A.
2. Your pupils are dilated.
3. C and D.
4. False.
5. True.

CHAPTER 5

HOW TO REACH YOUR GOAL

'A person without a goal is like a boat without a rudder.'
THOMAS CARLYLE

The Power Talk System is a method for *efficient* communicators. But what does efficient mean to you?

Are efficient communicators the ones who communicate successfully, or the ones who achieve their goals? Or is efficiency doing your best in the least amount of time?

Efficient ... efficient ... the word comes from 'effect': product the desired effect. I found the following description in a dictionary: 'An efficient person accomplishes a task successfully, and obtains the desired results.'

So we can agree that the definition of an efficient communicator is the person who attains his or her objective.

And what is the main cause of failure?

- Trouble being understood ...?
- Loss for words, especially when improvising ...?
- Stage-fright ...?
- Loss of memory ...?

No!

**The best way not to attain an objective
is to *forget to establish one*!**

One of the studies we conducted, with the help of a group of students, showed us that 96 per cent of public speakers do not have a precise objective, which they can summarise in one simple sentence, before they begin to speak.

If you only get one thing out of this book, let it be the following:

**Don't open your mouth to speak before you've set a
precise objective for yourself which you can summarise
in a single sentence.**

Because if you forget to set yourself an objective, your brain, which must have an objective in order to function, may decide on one that is completely different from the one you would have chosen.

When a conference or presentation is over, you might get the impression that nothing much happened. You couldn't say all you wanted, your marker ran out of ink, or you forgot to look at your audience . . . The important thing is, *did you attain your objective?*

You can always improve your presentation. The means aren't important. I've seen spectacular success, which violated all the principles in all the books. BUT THE SPEAKER HAD A GOAL. All his will-power was directed towards that goal, and the power of that person's personal magnetism increased tenfold.

Remember your first love affair. You had a goal. Spend an evening with your loved one, hold someone in your arms . . . we all know about that! Even if you were shy or clumsy, the power of your desire inspired you with ideas, courage, so that you got what you wanted (most of the time!).

This is the same type of thing. As soon as you set yourself a goal, summarise in a single sentence, ideas will come of themselves, your stage-fright will be transformed into courage, and whatever the means at your disposal, you will be *efficient*.

How does it work?

Look how important it is to have an objective. These are the thought processes involved:

- No objective → brain takes *fear* as an objective → failure, or
- No objective → brain chooses random objective → semi-failure.
- Multiple objectives → dispersed brain energy → semi-success.
- Precise objective → concentrated energy/supplementary brain activity → SUCCESS

To set an objective, begin by surveying the situation, just like you would examine a map to decide where you want to go.

The 3 factors of success

Your objective should take three factors into account: *you, the participants* and *the environment*. Where only two factors, exist, you have rapport. Build on it.

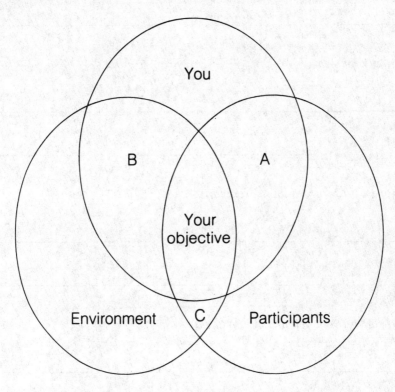

A good way to stimulate your creativity

Exercise
What points should you think about when considering:

You

_____

_____

Participants

_____

_____

The environment

_____

_____

Rapport between you and participants

_____

_____

Rapport between you and environment

_____

_____

Rapport between participants and environment

_____

_____

Solution
You You are the subject of this method! Think about your physical condition, your preparation, your subject, your understanding, your clothes, your gestures etc.

Participants Men or women? Average age? Number? Profession? Intellectual level? Points in common? Political or religious affiliation? Their psychology? How can you find out more about them? Do they know each other? What do they think about? Etc.

Environment Where will it take place? City? What kind of room? Size of the room? Technology available? Climate? A business? An organisation? Institution? Convention? Etc.

Rapport between you and participants Do you know them? How did you – or will you – meet? Are you adversaries or allies? Do you have any authority over them? What do they think of you? Inform yourself as necessary.

Rapport between you and environment What apparatus is at your disposal? Microphones? Screen? Audio-visual equipment? How can you set up the room to create a positive environment (music, posters, curtains etc.)? Where will you stand? Do you have everything you need? Are you informed about the region?

Rapport between participants and environment Are there one or a number of factors that could interfere with your presentation? Are they exterior (noise, movement etc.)? Is the telephone off the hook? What did the participants do before your presentation? The previous day? Are they at home or in a foreign environment? Etc.

When you've explored all these aspects, ask yourself the following question:

What do I want to obtain?

Write your answer, formulated as a *positive* sentence, at the top of a page. Don't write something like, 'I want our sales people to stop going over to the competition.' Instead write, 'I want our sales people to stay with us.'

If possible, formulate your goal *in the present*. It's more motivating to say, 'I want these people to contribute money to my project at the end of my conference' than to say 'I would like these people to contribute when they've finished listening to me.'

Use the first person. You'll feel more involved with an objective that mirrors the inner dialogue in your mind, than with 'A grant must be obtained . . .'

Set yourself an *active, concrete* and *precise* objective. 'Contribute money' is better than 'Help me.' 'Contribute a minimum of £50' is better than 'Contribute money.' 'Making them roll on the floor with laughter for ten minutes' is better than 'Amusing them . . .'

To conclude this chapter, read what happened to Mr Darby.

His uncle had a large plantation, which was tended by a number of black workers and their families, all of whom subsisted on what they harvested. One day, Darby went out to pay a visit to his workers. He was helping with the grinding of a quantity of wheat, when the door of the old mill opened and a little black girl entered and stood in the doorway. His uncle looked at the child and growled, 'What do you want?'

The little girl answered sweetly, 'My mama wants you to give her 50 cents.'

'Out of the question!' replied the uncle. 'Get out of here!'

'Yes, sir,' said the child. *But she didn't move.*

The uncle was so absorbed in his work that he didn't notice right away that the child was still there. But when he saw her, he shouted, 'What! Still here? Get out, or I'll throw you out!'

'Yes, sir,' said the child. *But she didn't budge.*

The uncle dropped the sack of grain he was pouring into the hopper, grabbed a barrel stave and walked up to the little girl menacingly. His anger was written all over his face.

Darby held his breath. He knew his uncle was not a man to be baited.

Staring him right in the eyes, the child took a quick step forward and shouted with all her might, 'My mama needs 50 cents!'

The uncle stopped dead in his tracks, looked at her for a long moment, then put down the stave, reached into his pocket and pulled out a half-dollar. The little girl took the money and backed right up to the door, without for a minute letting her gaze drop.

When she was gone, the uncle sat down on a box near the window and stared at the scenery for a good ten minutes. Shattered, he tried to figure out how he had been defeated by a little girl.

In the next chapter we look at how you should choose to talk about the subjects that are right for you. First, check how much you know about setting goals.

QUIZ

1. Being efficient means:
- [ ] **A** Working conscientiously.
- [ ] **B** Being prepared from the start.
- [ ] **C** Obtaining a desired effect.

2. What does your brain do if you don't set a precise objective?

☐ **A**   It adopts your fear as an objective.

☐ **B**   It adopts your momentary desires as an objective.

☐ **C**   It has no objective.

3. What rules should you follow to formulate a good objective?

☐ **A**   Phrase it in the *future* to show that it is an objective.

☐ **B**   Set a general objective, without being too precise, so that it includes all aspects of your motivation.

☐ **C**   Formulate it in a positive way.

☐ **D**   Start with 'It's important to . . .' to stimulate your will-power.

4. The three key elements to consider when setting your speech's objective are: (complete)

_____

_____

_____

Answers

1. C.

2. A and B.

3. C.

4. You; your participants; your environment.

CHAPTER 6

HOW TO GET IDEAS

'Don't work so hard. Put your feet up on the desk and look for ideas that will help our company make more money.'
JOHN ROCKEFELLER

You have probably read many books on positive thinking. And maybe you agree with the technique. But be careful.

Positive thinking is like a lottery: it creates a lot of hope for thousands of people, but very few come out winners. (As the saying goes, many are called, but few are chosen.) We're not saying it's completely useless, but for positive thinking to lead to success, there must be another ingredient. Just as flour without water will not make bread, positive thinking without *competence* will lead nowhere.

We've seen thousands of people – including some of our own staff – who refuse to make the effort to think and act, who want everything to fall right into their laps, ready-made. They want everything to be *easy* and *instantaneous*.

As you will see in the Power Talk System, preparation often counts for more than action. A project or theme should be so clearly defined in your mind that speaking about it becomes child's play, and getting ideas, arguments and outlines an easy and natural process.

Preparation: the key word

Whenever I watch Stephanie prepare for one of her conferences I am struck by her professionalism. She allows no room for error or failure – everything is thought out, planned, calculated – freeing her mind from worrisome details so that she can be relaxed and natural.

It's a little like this definition of culture: 'Culture is what remains when everything else has been forgotten.' Stephanie has mastered her subject so well, she is so competent, professional and prepared, that she can be completely relaxed and concentrate totally on her communication, and on the 65 per cent which we spoke about in previous chapters. But she speaks about subjects which are right for her.

How to choose subjects which are right for you

Dale Carnegie had an infallible method for determining whether or not a subject was suited to an individual:

> 'To find out whether or not you can handle a subject in public, ask yourself this question: if someone proposed the opposite point of view, would I be able to defend my own with conviction and passion? If so, then the subject is right for you.'

Unfortunately, there are many instances in professional life when a subject is imposed on you. If the subject is obligatory, while you remain indifferent, then *become a specialist*.

Ask yourself, out loud: 'Why do I have to make this presentation?'

If the answer is simply because your boss demands it of you, that's not enough. Every speech or oral presentation must have a goal. If you don't have an answer, find one. If you can't find any reasons for doing it, then keep quiet and refuse. You'll just waste your time – and the audience's time as well.

What to do when the subject is chosen for you

You can't say everything. Don't forget: your audience has only a limited capacity for assimilating what it hears. Just as when you want to photograph a spectacular landscape, you have to choose *a precise angle or point of view, the kind of lens*, and the *framing*, so in oral expression you have to frame your subject.

In some cases, to establish an initial consensus, you should point a 'wide-angle' lens at your subject. Allan Cayrol and Jo Saint Paul tell the following story in their book *Behind The Magic* (InterEditions, 1984):

> The director of a social service centre was constantly harassing his staff, as he waged a relentless war against tardiness, even down to the

minute. The rate of absenteeism and job rotation was especially high in his department.

When interrogated as to the goal of being so punctilious, he declared that punctuality is a sign that employees are interested in their work.

We reformulated his statement this way: If we understand you correctly, what you're saying is that the important thing for you is that your employees show an interest in their work.

He agreed. The employees also found this an acceptable requirement. So in this new frame, it was possible to find other means of assuring that the staff was motivated, and the objective was attained.

Once a German editor submitted a proposal to me, concerning publication of a book by P. K. Tepperwein called *Mental Self Healing*. When I thought about the title, I realised that most people know nothing about 'self-healing' and are not interested in mental exercises. So I renamed the book *Think and Heal*. Everybody thinks. And healing is something anyone with a health problem wants very badly.

A last example: I was once asked to give a conference on parapsychology – a vast subject! So I decided to focus on 'How to Develop Your Own Parapsychological Powers'. Framing the subject in this way made it more personal to the participants, more defined and easier to handle.

Exercise
Reframe the following subjects:

1. Communication

_____

_____

2. Techniques of buying and reselling property, and calculation of premiums

_____

_____

3. Sport

_____

_____

4. The science of dietetics in the twentieth century

_____

_____

5. Socio-cultural and religious habits of Nepal

_____

_____

Answers   (examples)
1. How to make friends and influence people
   Telephones and business
2. How to make a fortune in property
   How to buy your house
3. Sports and your health
   All the secrets of windsurfing
4. Bad meals
   Stay younger – live longer
5. Nepal: land of the gods
   Adventures on the 'Roof of the World'

How to exploit your subconscious for ideas

You need to have ideas before you can write them down.

Contrary to what many people think, most ideas are not born in the conscious, logical, Cartesian mind, but in the *subconscious*. The root of the word *idea* is to *see*. An idea comes from an image in the imagination.

The greatest discoveries are made during moments of reverie, when the subconscious germinates the conscious mind.

Kekulé solved the problem of the benzene molecule in a dream. Otto Loewi, Nobel prizewinner in medicine (1936), dreamed about his discovery one night. He wrote down a few notes so he would remember in the morning, but it was no use – he couldn't read his writing! Luckily, he had the same dream the following night, got up immediately and went to work.

Tartini wrote his 'Devil's Sonata' in a state of semi-somnabulism. Newton discovered the principle of universal gravitation after waking from a nap under an apple-tree. Béjart dreams his choreographies.

We could fill a book with examples. David Ogilvy (the renowned publicist) states that many of his ideas come to him in the bath. Mozart had the ideas for his symphonies while travelling in carriages. Edison, after working long hours on a solution, would take a little nap – and find the answer!

Putting your feet up on the desk, taking a bath, a nap or a short walk; these are all ways to tap into your subconscious.

How does the subconscious work?

Imagine a huge computer with three functions:

A. In which you must enter data (information)
B. To which you then ask a question.
C. Which answers at any moment, as soon as an answer is found.

That's just about how your subconscious works. Except that unlike man-made computers, the subconscious is capable not only of choosing ideas, but also of combining, discerning, guessing and predicting. In this light, it is superior to the conscious mind.

To be creative, to have ideas, you must use your subconscious in the same way you would use a vast, powerful computer with many times the capabilities of anything built by human hands.

A – Where to find the data – or information

When working on an oral presentation, explore all sources of information:

1. Your library and files, magazines, data libraries.

2. Encyclopaedias and dictionaries.

3. The press.

4. Public libraries and documentation centres.

5. People: colleagues, specialists, consultants, family, associates, friends, etc.

6. Seminars, conferences, training courses. etc.

7. Your personal experience (anecdotes, stories etc.) As Socrates said: 'All people are sufficiently eloquent to speak about what they know.'

How to work with your right brain

A fairly recent discovery in the field of creativity is the opposition of the right and left hemispheres of the brain.

We are used to depending mainly on the left brain, which is the seat of logic, conceptualisation, reason. In contrast, the important of the right brain, which is responsible for intuition, artistic talent, spirituality, spatial orientation etc., has been underestimated, and we are therefore not very adept at calling on its resources.

A young American writing teacher found a way to apply these insights into right-brain activity to facilitate his quest for ideas.

Right-brain thinking is not organised in a linear way: instead, it works in many directions at the same time. So making a list would be uncharacteristic of the right brain. To stimulate the right brain, we must represent our ideas *in space*, similar to the way they are processed in our head. Which leads to the idea of the tree.

You start by writing an initial idea in the centre of the page. Then you write all the main ideas which arise, and then all the secondary ideas which are connected to the main ideas, and so on.

On the next page you will find an example. The central idea is 'Memory'. We've just finished our research on the subject. You will have to admit that the 'tree' technique is more effective than a classical 'list'. It can often produce more than 30 per cent more ideas! Try it yourself and see.

One last word: if you don't have enough room for a series of branches that look promising, start another page. Write the connecting idea in the centre, and carry on from there.

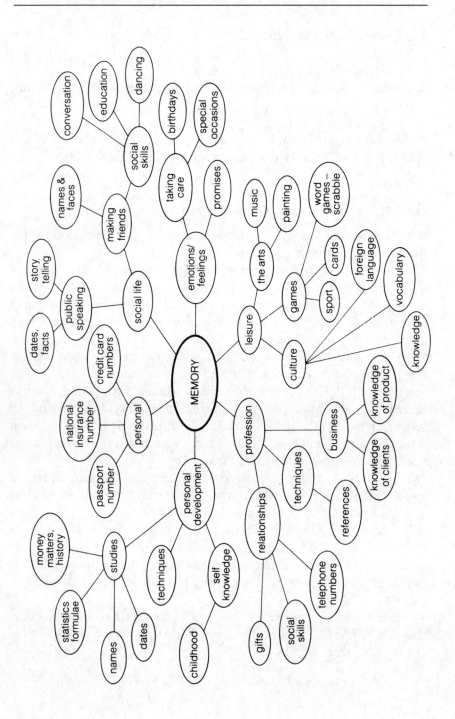

B – How to ask your subconscious a question

Take your objective, and phrase it *in the form of a question.*

A question is the best way to trigger your thinking. If you express your goal in the form of a statement, nothing will come in your mind. If you ask yourself a question, ideas will come like magic.

But try to summarise your objective in only one question. There's a story about a vicar who was training his son – who was a vicar as well – to deliver a moving sermon every Sunday by making him submit *a one-sentence summary* of his sermon the night before. Which the son dutifully did for a few months. Then one day the father received a two-page telegram which ended like this: 'Sorry, absolutely no time, could not prepare usual summary.'

It's easier to be *long-winded* than *short and precise*! Set yourself an objective, then phrase it in the form of a *question*. Here are some examples:

- How to convince the engineers to go ahead with my project before the summer holiday?
- How to motivate my sales people to double their gross sales by 15 March?
- How to announce a licensing decision without causing protests and resentment.
- How to obtain £30,000 from our parishioners to repair the roof of the church?
- How to convince my listeners to start their own direct-mailing business?

C – Wait for your subconscious to answer

When you've done all this, let your mind rest for a few days. Don't think about it any more. Your subconscious will go to work for you. The only thing you have to do is keep notes of the answers it provides. So you have to be ready, with pen and notebook handy, to write down whatever comes up, whether in the bathroom, in bed, in the car etc.

Don't put off making notes. As soon as an insight comes to you, write down the main points. If you don't you risk forgetting it, and losing it for good.

A last piece of advice: when we were children, we often would stare at our homework for hours, haunted by the thought that 'I'll never be able to do this.' If you let yourself be overcome by these kinds of thoughts, you will have a lot of trouble having ideas. Instead, tell yourself:

This is easy, and I can do it.

Try the quiz and see how much you already know.

QUIZ

1. Is positive thinking enough to assure success? Is there another essential ingredient? Which one?

_____

2. What sources of information should you access when preparing a presentation or speech?

_____

3. What is the '*tree*' technique?
- ☐ **A** A method of grafting used in agriculture.
- ☐ **B** A way to illuminate objects at night.
- ☐ **C** A way to find ideas.
- ☐ **D** A technique of using drawings as illustrations during a conference.

4. Here are three examples of a question that you can ask yourself in order to generate ideas and prepare a speech. Which is best?
- ☐ **A** How to obtain the staff's approval of and involvement in our new marketing strategy?
- ☐ **B** Why my marketing strategy is best for our company?
- ☐ **C** How to show simply and clearly all the details of our new marketing strategy?

Answers
1. Competence.
2. Encyclopaedias and dictionaries.
Press and related media.
Public libraries and documentation centres.
Your personal experience.
3. A way to find ideas using the power of your right brain.
4. A.

CHAPTER **7**

HOW TO STRUCTURE YOUR IDEAS

'The further away the place you want to reach, or the more complex the route, the more you need a detailed map. The same goes for communication. If you don't want to get lost − and lose your listeners as well − structure your ideas around a central plan.'

CHRISTIAN H. GODEFROY

How to sustain your audience's interest

Do you remember how images are connected in the brain? We saw that, in order to make new, unfamiliar concepts comprehensible, we have to relate them to already existing images.

There's another consideration. If you're always jumping from one train of thought to another, your listeners will not be able to organise the ideas you are trying to get across in a linear way. They will soon become disoriented, unable to follow you, and likely to lose interest.

So always be sure to present your ideas in an order that is *easy to follow*, so that your listeners can file them in the corresponding drawers of their brains without too much effort.

The key:

Put your ideas in order

should be learned by heart and applied by all the politicians, conference leaders and other communicators who are not able to get a clear message across.

Be clear. Don't we feel better when everything is in order, organised, in our homes and offices as well as in our heads?

12 proven formulas for planning a presentation

Before making a plan, when faced with the collection of ideas that you've accumulated, the first thing to do is to *regroup your ideas according to theme*, or central ideas.

Take some sheets of card and regroup all similar ideas around a central theme, one per sheet. There are also certain computer programs designed to do this work.

Once this is done, consider the different plans of approach that are possible, and decide which one is best suited to your subject.

1. Introduction/development/conclusion
This is the most classical of the classic approaches! What you should remember is the importance of the *introduction* and the *conclusion*. We'll be talking more about this in the following chapters. To save time, we will not cover the 'Introduction' and 'Conclusion' for all the other types of plan, but remember that *they are always necessary*.

2. Thesis/antithesis/synthesis
The thesis is the idea you want to promote; the antithesis is the exact opposite! The advantage of this approach is that it stimulates creativity and audience interest. Presenting the antithesis as well as the thesis also gives an impression of objectivity, which makes the synthesis at the end easier to accept. (But, of course, your antithesis should be weaker than your thesis.)

3. Problems/causes/solutions
This is a very simple plan, easy to follow, which corresponds to the way our brain functions. It is also the basis of the scientific method:

a. Awareness of a problem.
b. Study of facts and analysis of causes.
c. Possible solutions.
d. Testing possible solutions.
e. Choosing the best possible solution.

This approach is perfectly suited to rather lengthy presentations, where the audience is not partial to one or another point of view.

4. Cause/effect
From effect to cause, or cause to effect: this is deductive reasoning, which can have three stages:

All men are mortal
Socrates is a man
Therefore Socrates is mortal

There is also another order possible: effect → effect, without introducing the underlying causes. In this case, the first effect is known, while the second is probably, for example: 'If Christmas is warm, Easter will be cold.'

The plan which is based on Principle → Application is a variation of Cause → Effect.

5. Chronology

Chronological order is used mainly to tell a story. It can sometimes be broken (flashbacks, digressions etc.), to heighten dramatic effect.

A person's life story, for example, can be told in order of childhood, adolescence, adulthood, marriage etc. But the introduction could centre on the most dramatic moment in that person's life.

Processes are often described in chronological order: growth of a plant, or development of a product, for example.

6. Spatial organisation

Here, the logic works from 'near to far', or 'inside to outside', or the reverse. Presentations concerning voyages, explorations, vacations, expeditions etc. would be treated in this way (place, surrounding area, country etc.).

7. Definition

In this case, you explain a subject's *resemblances* and *differences* to other, familiar subjects. The subject is also examined in different contexts.

To maintain the interest of your listeners, it is advisable to adopt an original point of view.

For example, take desk top typesetting: first, point out the similarities with traditional typesetting (layout, characters, words). Then list the differences (vector characters merging text and graphics, speed, user friendly, etc.). Give your point of view, before/after, as a publisher or other interested party.

8. Classification

Here you enumerate points which fall into the same category. For example, 'The New Underprivileged Class in the Eighties'.

The plan is then split into parts. This approach is often called the 'filing cabinet plan'.

9. The Central Thread
Different elements are presented, and each is tied in to a 'central thread'.

A lawyer, wishing to expose a conspiracy against his client, would use this approach. Or an executive trying to explain why company sales dropped last year.

10. Example/argument/reason
This approach was developed by Dale Carnegie, and is especially suited to short presentations:

a. *Example* Start with a fact, a story that will act as the starting point of your presentation.
b. *Argument* In clear and precise terms, tell your audience exactly what you want of them.
c. *Reason* Reveal the benefits and advantages your audience can expect to gain.

11. Dialectic
Each solution is presented and rejected in turn. The initial problem and its demands are reformulated numerous times. The audience is left with only one possible solution.

This approach is mainly used to expound Marxist dogma.

12. Rudyard Kipling's plan
The famous writer said, 'Six faithful servants have taught me everything I know. They are called:
   Who?
   What?
   When?
   Where?
   Why?
   How?'
Ask these questions and provide the answers.

The best formula for persuading people

Adapted from our sales-letter formula, this approach has provided good results time and time again for commercial presentations:

1. Get your listeners *curious*.
2. Speak to them about *themselves*.

3. Show them what you are proposing *will do for them*.

4. Deliver your *message*.

5. *Prove* what you say.

6. *Summarise* your proposal.

7. Provide *good reasons* to act *right away*.

We will end this chapter with an approach suggested by an Irish politician:

'First say that you're going to say something, then say it, and finally SAY THAT YOU'VE SAID IT!'

QUIZ

1. How can you make sure that your listener follows your ideas?

_____

_____

_____

2. An introduction and conclusion:
- [ ] **A** Are not always necessary.
- [ ] **B** Are useful, but not indispensable.
- [ ] **C** Are necessary.
- [ ] **D** Are very important – often the most important parts of a presentation.

3. Which approach, which plan, should you use to tell a story?
- [ ] Thesis/antithesis/synthesis.
- [ ] Chronological.
- [ ] Central thread.

4. What are Rudyard Kipling's six faithful servants?

_____

_____

_____

_____

Answers

1. Put your ideas in order.

2. D.

3. Chronological.

4. Who? What? When? Where? Why? How?

CHAPTER 8

HOW TO MAKE YOUR
INTRODUCTION A SUCCESS

'An introduction must capture the listeners' attention, and prepare their minds for what will follow, without revealing too much.'
RUDOLPH FLESCH, author and communication expert

If you study commercials on TV, you will notice that often more than half the ad goes by *without the viewer knowing what the product is*. The objective is solely to *capture our attention*.

How to create a strong introduction

Here is a way to help you to find a good introduction: ask yourself questions – and not just any questions.

Working on the principle that the brain is mainly stimulated *by questions*, you will find your best introductions through an interrogative approach.

To make this chapter more interesting for yourself, choose a subject for communication.

Write it down here: _____

_____

3 rules for successful introductions

Now, try to answer each of the following questions, keeping in mind the objectives of a good introduction:

1. How to capture your listeners' attention?

2. How to create interest in the subject you're going to cover?

3. Introduce the subject?

9 proven techniques for introducing a subject

1. The Bettger technique

Frank Bettger, well-known author of *How I Went from Failure to Success*, used to ask questions like 'If it were possible for you to . . . (here you list an advantage) . . . would you be interested?'

Asking a question is a good introduction technique. Now look at your subject and think about the kinds of questions you could use as an introduction. Here are a few hints:

> If it were possible for you to . . .?
> Would you like to . . .?
> Do you own a . . .?
> Do you have a . . .?
> Do you know that . . .?
> Do you know people who . . .?
> Could you imagine . . .?
> Has it ever happened to you that . . .?
> How much did you pay for . . .?
> Haven't you ever felt . . .?
> How many times have you asked yourself . . .?
> What is . . .?
> Are you . . .?
> What would you say if . . .?
> What do you think about . . .?
> Isn't it strange that . . .?
> Have you ever noticed . . .?
> Is it true that . . .?

2. Novelty

Here the key starting words are 'Now . . .' 'At last . . .' 'A new . . .' 'Good news . . .' 'Everyone is talking about . . .' 'has just been . . .'.

Ask yourself the question:

What news will I announce in my introduction?

3. The striking idea

If you examine TV commercials, you can study the kinds of introductions used by the pros to interest you in their product.

They know very well how important introductions are, and devote enormous amounts of energy and care to creating them. As David Ogilvy, the advertising genius, said: 'If you screw up the introduction, the client wastes 80 per cent of his money . . .'

Ask yourself the question:

**Is there a way to start my presentation
with an original, striking idea?**

4. The summary

You can be almost sure not to go wrong with this technique: it consists of summarising your proposal, of expressing in a few words all the advantages, so that you arouse your listeners' desire to know more – in other words, you make them drool.

It's a little like going to a chic restaurant where you can see all the different dishes attractively displayed before you start eating. You smell the aroma, and can't wait to get started.

**What advantages should be mentioned in the summary to
arouse the curiosity and interest of my listeners?**

5. Imagination

'Imagine. It's two o'clock in the morning. You're sleeping soundly, when suddenly . . .'

The advantage of this approach is that it implicates your audience in some kind of *action*.

**How can I get my listeners involved in an action
by starting with, 'Imagine . . .'**

6. Personalisation

In this kind of introduction, your address each member of the audience directly, citing characteristics which relate to them personally. For example, if you're giving a conference on 'How to Start Your Own Business' you could say something like, 'People like you have become rare enough . . .' or 'You belong to that small group of people who possess initiative and the will-power to succeed.'

Ask yourself the question:

How can I personalise my introduction?

7. Personal testimonial

Listen to what Maurice Ogier, a specialist in communication, has to say:

The best introduction: talk about a personal experience.

As insignificant as it may seem, a story that you have experienced yourself is the *best way* to *capture* attention, because everybody likes a good story.

If your story is closely related to your subject, it will serve as an excellent *hook*, bringing your audience directly to the heart of the matter.

So start by telling some personal anecdote, with a lot of images and details, as insignificant as that anecdote may seem: you will be doubly rewarded:

- On the one hand, it's *easy* to tell about something that you've lived yourself; and you will appreciate this when you begin speaking, since it is an effective way to combat stage-fright.
- On the other hand, you will *interest* your audience; and that's your primary objective.

Ask yourself the question:?

What personal anecdote can I use as an introduction to captivate my audience?

8. The story

Anything can be presented in the form of a story. Rudolph Flesch, an expert on efficient public speaking, and the author of several books, goes so far as to say that it's *only* stories that people are interested in. So equip yourself with a notebook in which you can jot down any interesting stories you hear on the radio or TV, that you can read, or that other people tell you.

Don't forget to note the *details*. It's names, dates, places and precise facts that bring life to a story.

What moving story can I tell to introduce my subject?

9. The quotation

When you read a book, *underline* the interesting passages. If necessary, copy them into files, which you can classify by theme.

Add to your files by clipping interviews from magazines and newspapers, and finding quotes in dictionaries and encyclopaedias.

A citation will be more effective if it comes from someone who is known and respected by your audience.

What quotation could I use for my introduction?

Sometimes, start a speech with a *funny story*. This serves to create a relaxed atmosphere right away. But this technique can be a double-edged sword if the story has nothing to do with what follows. So you should always subtly relate the funny story to the subject you have chosen.

If you like, you can use *more than one kind of introduction simultaneously*.

For example, tell a story as a personal experience and add an original hook at the end:

> On 25 February 1975, a police officer came to my home, looking for me. He gave me no explanation, and demanded that I accompany him to a garage at the end of a deserted street.
>
> 'Has this car ever belonged to you?' he asked, pointing to a slightly damaged, recent model Porsche 911T.
>
> 'No, never.' The officer seemed to relax. Then he explained that my Porsche, which I'd sold three months before, had been scrapped and dumped in the river, and that someone had tried to use my papers to sell the car I'd just seen, which had been stolen.
>
> The officer then stated, 'About fifty people a day buy a stolen car without knowing it. Not only do we confiscate the vehicle, but the buyer loses his money, and is sometimes charged with aiding a felon!'

This introduction was used in a speech about the dangers of buying a used car.

7 faults to avoid

The most common faults are:

- Being negative.
- Excusing yourself (for not being ready, or a good enough speaker, or not having enough time etc.).
- Making the introduction of the subject-matter too long.
- Putting on an air of superiority, or making your audience feel that you're much more knowledgeable than they are.

- Being (or appearing to be) confused.
- Leaving out a *real* introduction ('Well, it's time to start ... everyone seems to be here ... Well, I'd like to talk about ...').
- Stripping the subject of interest by revealing too much too soon. Maintain an aura of mystery. Stimulate your listeners' curiosity.

As a priest once said, 'When the congregation is falling asleep, get the beadle to take a sharp stick and prick the preacher!'

Study the quiz to see how well you have mastered the art of the introduction. Next we look at the often most important part of your speech – the conclusion.

QUIZ

1. The aims of a good introduction are to:
- ☐ **A** Introduce the subject.
- ☐ **B** Tell your audience what you expect of them.
- ☐ **C** Capture your listeners' attention.
- ☐ **D** Capture attention at all costs, even if it has nothing to do with what follows.

2. The introduction's first step is:
- ☐ Introducing yourself.
- ☐ Introducing the subject.
- ☐ Thanking participants for being here.
- ☐ Capturing attention.

3. Among the kinds of introduction technqiues, we find:
- ☐ **A** The Summary.
- ☐ **B** The Category.
- ☐ **C** The Personalisation.
- ☐ **D** The Binding Thread.

4. People are interested only by
- ☐ Theories.
- ☐ Facts.
- ☐ Stories.
- ☐ Statistics.

5. In an introduction, you should avoid:
- ☐ **A** Summarising the advantages.
- ☐ **B** Being confused.
- ☐ **C** Assuming an air of superiority.

Answers
1. A and C.
2. Capture attention.
3. A and C.
4. Stories.
5. B and C.

CHAPTER **9**

How to Make Your Conclusion a Success

'Oh, well, I haven't got it all worked out in my head. Just the general idea, and exactly how I'm going to end.'
GEORGE F. JOHNSON, professional speaker

Imagine: you've just finished your presentation. You've said your last word, and now you're waiting for the applause.

Nothing. Total silence. You could hear a pin drop.

You stand there, a sheepish grin on your face, wondering what you did or didn't do – how you could have failed so miserably.

Your conclusion! A *good* conclusion – and we've experienced this ourselves – can result in a standing ovation, and a torrent of congratulations!

5 basic elements of a good conclusion

We do not believe in the predominance of the left side of the brain, especially as far as speaking in public is concerned: people are ruled by emotion more than by logic. It's fine to organise your thoughts in an ordered way, but remember that the two most important moments are:

Your introduction ... and your conclusion.

The chances are that your audience will forget most of the rest of what you say.

In your opinion, what basic elements constitute a good conclusion?

Answer A good conclusion has the following qualities:

1. Simple language;
2. Imagery;
3. Curiosity and interest are aroused more than ever;
4. The subject is reiterated, or summarised;

And, above all:

5. *The very last sentence must be the clearest, simplest, most striking set of words imaginable.*

It's a little like dotting your i's. You shove a last piece of irrefutable and amazing evidence right up under the noses of your listeners, so that they *must* think, *must* agree, *must* act.

You should work on your last sentence over and over again until you're satisfied. You won't regret it!

What to avoid?

Before looking at the best techniques for concluding a presentation or a speech, here are some points to avoid:

- Dragging it out.
- Sudden speeding up or ending because of lack of time.
- Negative or redundant statements.
- Statements that leave room for *doubt* (If . . . Maybe . . . I hope . . .).
- Excuses and justifications.
- Extended conclusions: the audience is ready to applaud, but the speaker starts talking again!
- Not stopping, being afraid of silence, rambling on without knowing what to say (Are there any more questions . . .?).
- 'Thank you for your time and attention' (Better than nothing, but should be avoided) or 'That's all, I have nothing more to say' (which is worse).
- If you allow a question period, forgetting to add a second conclusion at the end.

Practise your conclusions by speaking into a tape recorder or in front of a friend. Listen to yourself while you are speaking and learn to recognise when you are in danger of lessening the impact or effectiveness of your final words.

7 stimulating conclusions

Now look at some examples of good conclusions:

1. The summary conclusion

It's often a good idea to conclude a presentation or speech by summarising what you've said − especially if your subject was in any way complex.

Conclusions of this type usually start with key expressions such as:

In short − therefore − in conclusion − so, to summarise − let's remember that − to conclude − etc.

To practise this type of conclusion, you can summarise articles or chapters of books that you read. In a short time, you will learn to *get right to what is essential*.

Try it with the following text:

An Initiation to Action
There are certain conditions where we can make decisions, but are incapable of carrying them out. These conditions result from extreme fatigue, alcoholism, low blood pressure, low blood sugar levels, brain lesions or hypnosis.

A person drinks too much and then goes home. He lies down on a couch, reads a little, and wants to go to sleep. But two hours later, he's still on the couch, saying he should get to sleep.

Studies conducted on high altitude pilots show that a similar condition can result from lack of oxygen. Pilots who wait too long to supplement their oxygen intake become incapable of doing so at all, even though they are conscious, and know that they should.

A mine inspector, trapped in a fall, wrote a farewell letter to his wife while slowly being asphyxiated by carbon monoxide. The letter was incoherent and repetitive, and didn't make sense. What is interesting to us here is that the inspector knew very well that he could save his life by crawling another twenty yards forward. But he'd lost the ability to make the necessary movements.

In relation to our study of will-power, the problem is knowing exactly how we undertake appropriate actions once a decision has been made.

(Professor N. L. Munn, *Treatise on Psychology*)

Now your conclusion − summary:

Sample answer To summarise, will-power is *necessary* to action, but it is not *sufficient*. We must also possess the *power to transform thought into action*.

2. Reiterative conclusions (repeat the message)

The easiest way to conclude is to repeat the central idea of your presentation or argument.

In this type of conclusion, the central idea is repeated, almost like a *slogan*:

Indifference is gaining ground – WE MUST ACT NOW.
If you're not part of the solution, you're part of the problem.
We have to start taking care of city hall, before city hall takes care of us.
Every journey starts with a single step.

3. Perspective conclusions

These conclusions open new perspectives for the listeners. Here are some examples:

At the speed present research is going, we can expect that in twenty years . . .
In the future you will HAVE TO deal with these kinds of problems . . .
Japan and the US have already adopted the system with great success. Studies here are well under way, and experts predict it will soon be in place in major urban centres across the country.

4. Inciting conclusions

These conclusions incite people to *act*, and are often fused with a summary conclusion, as this example shows:

In short gentlemen, laboratory tests have been carried out in the United States, Switzerland and Germany; the large gains this product will mean, as well as the greater security it represents for us all, lead me to advise you to approve the project before our competitors have an opportunity to access rights and licences. We must sign the contract next week or be left behind.

Another example:

. . . During this exposition you can take advantage of a 20 per cent reduction and receive a free gift. See the hostess on the way out, and fill in the form she has for you. It'll be your best buy of the year.

Dale Carnegie, in his book *How to Speak in Public*, states:

The last words spoken in a conference should incite people to ACT. Don't hesitate. Tell your audience to contribute, vote, write, call, buy, protest, investigate, acquire . . . anything you like. But take some elementary precautions:

- ASK FOR SOMETHING PRECISE (. . .)

- ASK YOUR AUDIENCE FOR SOMETHING THEY *CAN* GIVE YOU

- MAKE IT AS EASY AS POSSIBLE FOR YOUR AUDIENCE TO MEET YOUR DEMAND(S)

5. The challenge-question

To conclude, the question we must all face is this: do we have the courage to vote this project down? Yes or no! Or do we approve it, like a bunch of sheep?

Is there room in your heart to help these tragic, unfortunate human beings?

6. The quotation

Remember Plato's astute comment: 'By ignoring public affairs, the so-called wise man punishes himself by allowing himself to be governed by other men who are not wise.'

As Molière liked to say: 'I hate the faint-hearted who, in the guise of not wishing to offend, never dare undertake anything.'

7. The example or anecdote

You can choose a story that illustrates and summarises your proposal. Make sure that the point of the story is clear.

You can also use a personal anecdote:

> And as my foot touched the ground, everything seemed unreal – the smell of the grass, the fresh breeze, the lights. Since that day, I've never forgotten that life is a precious gift that we must merit, and that it's action, and action alone, that leads us to success.

Final advice on conclusions

1. Don't try to come up with a good conclusion until you've fully mastered your subject. The same goes for the introduction. That's why, in this book, we have covered introductions and conclusions *after* planning and development.
2. End on a note of maximum emotional intensity. Change your physical attitude. Mobilise all your energy. The key word is POWER!
3. After your conclusion, sit down. Leave the stage. Let your physical behaviour make it clear that you're finished. If you leave room for doubt, if you hesitate, your conclusion will not work.
4. Engrave this formula for success in your mind:

CONCLUSION = POWER + EMOTION + CONVICTION

QUIZ

1. The last sentence of your talk should be as clear, simple and . . . . . . as possible.

2. In a good conclusion, you should *avoid*:
   - [ ] **A** Excuses and justifications.
   - [ ] **B** Thanks.
   - [ ] **C** Predictions.
   - [ ] **D** Rambling on.

3. The most important part of a conclusion is:
   - [ ] **A** The summary of what was said.
   - [ ] **B** Thanking the audience.
   - [ ] **C** The last sentence.
   - [ ] **D** Waiting for applause.

4. The conclusion of your speeches should:

- ☐ **A** Be long, in order to hold the attention of your audience.
- ☐ **B** Be the place where you apologise if something went wrong during the conference.
- ☐ **C** Be a question-and-answer session.
- ☐ **D** Give the impression that everything is finished, in order to be applauded, and then you can give the real conclusion.

Answers

1. Striking.

2. A and D.

3. C.

4. None of these answers is true.

PART 2

How to convince people without creating opposition – and win the enthusiastic co-operation of your listeners

CHAPTER 10

HOW TO BE A 'PSYCHOLOGIST'

'You can only talk to a hungry man in terms of bread.'
MAHATMA GANDHI

6 rules to get your audience to like you

You have to give to receive. That's a fundamental law of life. If you want your audience to be friendly towards you, you must *first treat them like friends*. If you're afraid of them, if you treat them like enemies, they will sense your attitude and will, in effect, become your enemies.

This may remind you of Dale Carnegie's six rules, which are so central to his book *How to Make Friends and Influence People*:

Rule 1 **Be sincerely interested in others.**

Rule 2 **Smile!**

Rule 3 **Remember that someone's name is, for that person, the sweetest-sounding and most important word in his or her entire vocabulary!**

Rule 4 **Learn to listen. Encourage people to talk about themselves.**

Rule 5 **Talk to your listeners about what they like to hear.**

Rule 6 **Make your listeners feel really important.**

Let's look more closely at each of these rules:

Rule 1

The key word here is 'sincerely'. People can detect the difference between someone who is feigning interest and someone who is *sincerely* interested in them. Ask questions. Imagine you're a journalist writing an article about the person you're speaking to. Sincerity comes from the heart. Tune in to your audience.

Rule 2

Smile. You know how a smile can light up a face. Well, your face is no different. Your eyes shine when you smile. You become attractive. Of course, I'm talking not about a forced smile but about a real smile that is pleasing to others and makes you a person they want to like.

Rule 3

What could be more embarrassing than forgetting or mixing up the name of a person you are talking to? Each person considers his or her name to be very precious, whether they know it or not. It is a symbol, which represents their entire being. Forget it, or confuse it with someone else's, and you make yourself an enemy!

Rule 4

It isn't easy to listen to people, because most of us are more interested in ourselves than in others. Remember that you have two ears and only one mouth. Use them proportionally! To encourage others to talk about themselves, reinforce their communication by nods of the head and short messages like 'Oh yes,' 'Really' 'And then?' 'Incredible!' etc.

Rule 5

Dale Carnegie was surprised by the fact that, although he adored strawberries and cream, he had to use something else as bait when trying to attract fish to bite his hook! You might be fascinated by a certain subject. And you think whatever you have to say about it is very interesting. But you'll be a lot more interesting *if you speak about what your listeners like.*

Rule 6

All people have doubts about themselves, at least in certain areas. We all need to be reassured, to feel that we're somehow important to those around us. Naturally, we feel we're important to the people we like. So make your listeners aware of how important they are to you. Try to dispel their innate shyness. And I'm talking not about servile flattery but about sincere compliments. Look for people's virtues instead of their faults.

How to develop your empathy

Here's an imposing word: *empathy*. Its Greek root means 'feel like'. Empathy can be defined as 'the imaginary projection of one individual's awareness to another'.

Don't start thinking that empathy is an exercise in telepathy or hypnosis. No. It's a quality which you already possess, and which you only have to learn to develop.

In simple terms, empathy is the acquired ability to completely understand someone else's point of view. Or, more accurately, to project your imagination, to put yourself in someone else's shoes, to see things from another person's point of view. For example, have you ever helped your favourite tennis player return a difficult shot, while watching from the stands or on TV?

There's a world of difference between the poor little ego-centred person, concerned only with himself, and the outgoing, likeable, expansive and altruistic type whom everyone would like to get to know.

6 ways to improve your empathy

Here are a few methods which have worked for us;

1. *Take advantage of any opportunities that might arise to speak to all kinds of people.* And, if possible, *listen* more than you speak.

   If you take a taxi, talk to the taxi-driver. Talk to your cleaning lady, to the caretaker, the postman, shopkeepers . . . everyone with whom you come in contact.

   Listen to what they have to say, and try to understand their point of view, their preoccupations, their problems. Their mental universes are different from yours: try to broaden your own understanding of human nature by getting to know what they are thinking, and why.

Meanwhile, you absolutely must stop that machine in your head that is always criticising. You must learn to *accept people as they are.*

2. *Vary your reading.* Read magazines and newspapers with large circulations, even if you consider them beneath your intellectual level.

3. *Build yourself an image* of the people to whom you are speaking. Think about those people's day-to-day existence, their work, what they do with their leisure time, their centres of interest, what they read, what they're worried about. *Put yourself in their shoes.*

4. *Have the text of your presentation read (or read it yourself) by a variety of people,* if possible by people whose background is different from your own. Listen to their comments attentively, and don't reject what they have to say before carefully considering their point of view.

5. Remember that when you *exchange your viewpoint* with that of someone else, you are both *benefitting* from the experience. You will not lose anything by sharing your point of view with someone else. On the contrary: you still have your own point of view, you have another's point of view as well and, what's more, the discussion arising from these different view-points often leads to interesting new ideas which you wouldn't have thought of yourself.

6. In conversation, get into the habit of summarising what someone tells you, and asking if *that's really what he or she wanted to say.* This is an excellent way to exercise empathy.

What makes people act?

Nothing is stranger than human behaviour, than all the things men and women do. No two people act in exactly the same way. And yet, in a larger sense, everyone acts in order to satisfy their own needs.

What are these needs?

Abraham Maslow, a well-known American psychologist, conducted a study on the subject of human needs, and came up with a chart in the form of a ladder, called 'Maslow's Ladder'.

5 questions to ask yourself in order to live up to your listeners' expectations

Why is Maslow's chart called a 'ladder'? Because needs appear as a progression. In general terms, the essential, basic needs must be satisfied before more abstract, complex needs appear.

THE PHYSIOLOGICAL NEEDS

As Gandhi said, you can only talk to a hungry man in terms of bread. People's behaviour changes when they are really hungry: their perceptions change (they see and smell food with greater intensity); their memories of foods and tastes improve and they are capable of recalling a good meal in amazing detail.

Their emotions change. They become more tense and nervous until their craving for food is satisfied. Their thoughts, fantasies and dreams are all oriented towards food. I remember on the fifth day of a raisin diet I followed – I ate nothing but raisins for ten days – dreaming all night long of steak and chips.

If you observe people who are hungry, you will see that food is their sole desire, their only need, and occupies all of their conscious thinking.

Another physiological need is breathing. If people are deprived of air, they will do anything to get it. All other needs disappear from their minds: they must breathe at any cost.

A person who is deprived of air, food and/or water is capable of killing to satisfy his or her physiological needs.

Think about people who are shipwrecked or lost at sea and turn to cannibalism to survive. An act which seems horrible, inconceivable, impossible under normal circumstances becomes comprehensible under certain conditions, when people are no longer capable of satisfying their physiological needs.

Imagine that you are Robinson Crusoe. You've just been thrown up on the shores of a desert island, half-naked and exhausted. What are your immediate needs? The answer to this question will provide you with a pretty complete list of your physiological needs.

Someone who is in pain will need *to soothe the pain and avoid more discomfort*. If a person has to urinate, or defecate . . .

Someone who is tired needs *sleep*. Someone who is cold needs to get warm *to maintain normal body temperature* (by finding clothes, shelter, making a fire etc.)

First *hunger* and *thirst*. Then *sexual* needs. The concept of homoeostasis is a model which explains how physiological needs work. This is an automatic regulating system in the body. If you lack salt in your blood, or water, you will *crave* salt or water. If you lack sugar, you will want to eat something sweet, like a fruit etc.

But researchers have found that there are other physiological needs: the need for light, noise (total silence is insupportable, and causes hallucinations), the need to touch and feel etc.

Someone who has been prevented from satisfying one or another physiological need can be affected for the rest of his or her life. Someone who has known real hunger may organise his or her life around the motivating force of always having enough to eat, and never having to face the horror of starvation again.

Let's get back to the example of Robinson Crusoe. You have slept, you've found shelter, you've eaten some fruit and you are no longer hungry.

What would your desires be now?

To *predict* the satisfaction of your future physiological needs – in other words, *security*.

THE NEED FOR SECURITY

THE PHYSIOLOGICAL NEEDS

Still with our example of Robinson Crusoe, you would look for *clothes*, you'd build yourself some kind of *cabin*, you'd gather *a stock of* provisions, you would built a defence system to *protect* yourself from wild animals, you would look for weapons to *defend* yourself, you would try to cultivate a variety of foods to prevent illness.

Maslow describes security needs in this way:

> If the physiological needs are relatively well taken care of, a new series of needs arises: security, stability, protection, freedom from fear, anxiety, chaos; the need for structure, order, laws and limits, to be protected by someone who is strong etc.

Despite the fact that our society is extremely well organised in this area (consider social security programmes, medical and other forms of insurance, the police and all the official bodies which control and reassure us), we can still observe that the need for security is extremely strong. You only have to listen to some of the campaign speeches made by politicians running for office, and observe the kinds of promises that they make, to understand that the need for security is an extremely powerful motivating force.

A large proportion of the objects that you're surrounded with are the results of your desire for security. From refrigerators to locks to medicine cabinets, you are equipping yourself to assure your future security.

Meanwhile, you might have noticed that some things fulfil two functions: physiological needs and the need for security. To own a house, for example, protects you from outside aggressions (weather, intruders, etc.) *now* and in the *future*.

As soon as crisis or unsettling situations arise (war, economic depression, crime waves, social upheavals, natural catastrophes etc.), these needs become more pressing.

So you're Robinson Crusoe again. Once you get yourself organised, you start to get bored. And that's when 'Friday' comes along.

```
THE NEED FOR LOVE
AND BELONGING
```

```
THE NEED FOR SECURITY
```

```
THE PHYSIOLOGICAL NEEDS
```

Most people, once their initial series of needs have been satisfied, being to 'hunger' for relations with others; they hunger for affection, love, friendship, a companion. They crave a place in a group or family. Although these needs may be absent while more essential requirements are lacking, they surface as soon as these requirements are obtained, so people suffer acutely from *solitude*, feelings of being *rejected*, not having any *friends* or *roots* and lack of *tenderness* and *love* in their lives.

And we mustn't confuse love with sexuality, even though the two notions are intimately connected. Love implies giving and taking, with an undercurrent of affection which is not purely physical. A sexual need can be satisfied through masturbation, but that will not fulfil the desire to be loved.

In the face of danger, these feelings are heightened. Loyalty and camaraderie in the face of death, self-sacrifice and heroic deeds are not uncommon among soldiers on the battlefield, as well as among street gangs, the police, terrorist organisations etc.

The beginnings of 'fashion', the separation of people into groups and classes, is based on this need.

Publicity in general, and direct sales in particular, fully exploit the motivating forces created by this need. We need to feel valued by ourselves, and to be recognised and appreciated by others.

```
┌─────────────────────┐
│ THE NEED FOR        │
│ RECOGNITION         │
└─────────────────────┘
```

```
┌──────────────────────────┐
│ THE NEED FOR LOVE        │
│ AND BELONGING            │
└──────────────────────────┘
```

```
┌────────────────────────────┐
│ THE NEED FOR SECURITY      │
└────────────────────────────┘
```

```
┌──────────────────────────────┐
│ THE PHYSIOLOGICAL NEEDS      │
└──────────────────────────────┘
```

Maslow describes the need for recognition as follows:

> Above all, there is a need for power, for accomplishment, for mastery and competence, for confidence in our own prowess in the face of the vast world around us, for independence and freedom. Following these, we have what we call the desire for reputation or prestige.

Nothing is more unbearable than the dullness of anonymity.

There have been cases where people have gone so far as to commit murder just to get their names printed in the newspaper.

Even if you have fulfilled all your desires, satisfied all your needs, you will still be left with a last 'motivating dissatisfaction' at the bottom of your heart, which will lead you to action: *the need to exploit your potential.*

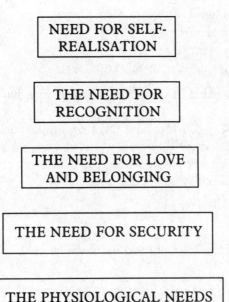

Maslow describes the need for self-realisation like this: 'Whatever a man *can* be, he *must* be.'

This refers to artists who succeed in transforming their ideas into reality, to inventors and creators as well as to the persons who create and invent their own lives. Instead of following the path of conformity, they find new ways to solve their problems and be happy. For example, an executive can persuade his boss to let him work at home with his fax and computer in order that he can avoid the traffic jams and see more of his family. Somebody who loves to swim can move his company to a seaside location. And so on.

As long as we are still caught up with the more mundane levels of needs, it is hard to imagine a person whose sole aim is to realise fully his or her potential.

We often reach this stage, but only partially. We might get closer to it when we're on holiday, for example, or during our leisure time.

Meeting your audience's needs

When you have to speak in front of a group, ask yourself the following questions:

1. Who are these people? (see Chapter 5)

2. Why are they here?

3. What forces motivate them?

4. What do they want from me?

5. What do I have to offer them? (see Chapter 5)

If you keep their needs in your mind, it will ensure that you fulfil them in your speech.

Next you need to consider how you are going to talk to your audience. Have you thought about the actual words you are going to use? How you are going to attract your audience to you? Before you consider such ideas, think carefully about what you have just read.

QUIZ

1. Give some of the rules of good human relations.

_____

_____

_____

_____

_____

2. What is empathy?

☐ **A** Finding somebody nice.

☐ **B** A form of sickness.

☐ **C** A way to control others.

3. What are the basic needs of humans?

Need for _____

Need for _____

Need for _____

Need for _____

Need for _____

Answers

1. Be sincerely interested in others.

Smile.

Remember that a person's name is the sweetest and most important word in his or her vocabulary.

Know how to listen.

Make people feel that you sincerely think they are important.
2. Empathy is the imaginary projection of the mind of one individual into another.
3. Self-realisation.
   Recognition.
   Love and belonging.
   Security.
   Physiological.

CHAPTER **11**

'GOLDEN' WORDS – AND FORBIDDEN WORDS

'Great Spirit, help me never to judge another before wearing his moccasins for at least three weeks.'

AMERICAN INDIAN PRAYER

The 'golden' words

Imagine that I take out a Polaroid camera and ask you and your family to step forward. I arrange you in a group, and then ... FLASH! A few seconds later the picture comes out, perfectly developed.

I then pass the picture around, and ask you to have a good look at it.

What will be the first thing you do when you get the picture?

You would look for yourself, for what kind of expression you had, and *then* look at the others.

Why?

Take a few seconds to think about it.

Answer Because, as one of the golden rules of communication states, people are interested FIRST AND FOREMOST IN THEMSELVES.

If people are mostly interested in themselves, how should you talk to them? Which words will they most like to hear?

- You
- Your
- Yours
- Yourself
- Yourselves.

We'll call these our *'Golden Words'*.

The 'forbidden' words

Now let's look at the negative words. Which words are most likely to alienate or strain your audience?

Answer
- I
- Me
- My
- Mine
- We
- Us
- Our
- Ours
- Ourself
- Ourselves.

We'll call these the '*Forbidden*' *Words*.

There is an exception, however: when you recount a personal experience that is interesting to your listeners, in other words, when you *expose yourself*. This is the time you can talk about yourself because your audience will be able to identify with you.

Also, when you are part of the same group as your audience, you can use 'we' or 'us'. We or us become 'golden' words.

'Forbidden' *versus* 'golden'

In order to visualise the effect of these words, imagine this scene:

You are speaking in front of a group. Whenever you use a 'forbidden' word, *the group takes a step backwards*. Whenever you use a 'golden' word, *the group takes half a step forward*.

When we try this experiment in our seminars, a number of speakers find themselves standing in an empty room after only a few sentences. Others have to be stopped before they get trampled, so attractive were their speeches. Still others provoke no reaction at all. They do not use one personal word.

If a speaker uses neither a golden nor a forbidden word for longer than three or four minutes, the group starts to get very bored.

For most speakers it is very difficult not to use forbidden words, even though they know what the result will be. Why not try, every time you speak in public, to see – in your imagination, of course – your audience stepping back when you use forbidden words, and coming closer when you use golden words.

The Egometer

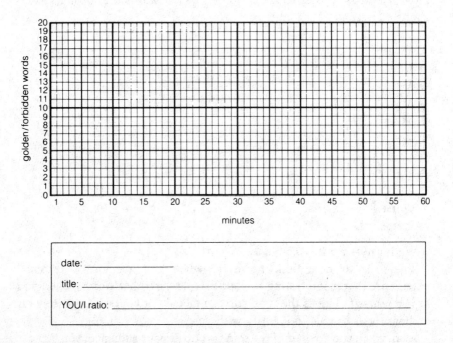

Look at the graph above.

The next time you speak in public, *tape yourself*. Then take a stopwatch, and count the number of times you use golden and forbidden words each minute.

Note your results on the graph. The numbers along the bottom represent minutes, while the numbers on the left are for golden – or forbidden – words. Now draw a curve in red for the forbidden words, and one in black for the golden words.

What do *you* score on the egometer?

Exercise

In the following text, underline the golden words and circle the forbidden words. Then transfer your findings to the egometer. To facilitate the timing aspect, I have entered a symbol ▷ after every five or six lines to indicate one minute of time passed.

Headquarters, Milan, 1st Prairial, Year IV (20 May 1796).
Men of Arms!

You are positioned, like a torrent on a mountaintop, ready to strike; you have routed, dispersed and scattered everything and everyone who dared stand in the way of your advance. Piedmont, liberated from the Austrian tyranny, has been restored to its natural attitude of peace and friendship towards France. ▷

Milan is yours, and the flags of the Republic are raised high throughout the whole of Lombardy. The Dukes of Parma and Modena owe their political survival to your compassion and generosity. The armies which seemed so threatening, bloated with false pride and assurances of help, now find themselves defenceless against your courage and might. ▷

The Po, the Tessin, the Adda, could not stop your tide even for a single day; you have proven these famed lines of Italian defence inadequate, crossing them as quickly as you did the Apennine range. Your magnificent success has brought joy to the heart of the homeland; a national holiday has been declared to celebrate your victories, in all corners of the Republic. ▷

Your mothers, fathers, wives, your sisters and lovers all rejoice over your success, and speak proudly about their love for you.

Yes, men, you have accomplished a lot: but is there nothing left for you to do? Will we let it be said that we knew how to be victorious, but that we didn't know how to profit from victory? ▷

Will we allow posterity to blame us for failing in Lombardy? No! I see you already running to take up your arms: throw off your fatigue: each moment you waste is more lost glory and happiness! So let us move onward! We still have days of forced march ahead of us, enemies to conquer, laurels to gather, and injuries to rectify. ▷

Let those who have sharpened the blades of civil revolt in France, those cowards who have assassinated our ministers and burned our servants in Toulon, let those traitors beware: the hour of revenge is at hand.

But let the people rest assured that we are their friends, that we wish them no harm, that we respect them as descendants of those great models of justice and freedom from tyranny, Brutus and Scipion. ▷

Your task is to re-establish the Capitol, to honour the statues of those revered heroes and martyrs who made the Roman people famous, to awaken them from their stupor, numbed as they are by centuries of slavery. These will be the fruits of your victory. Your deeds will be recorded for all posterity. You will merit immortal glory, for having changed the destiny of the most beautiful and ancient part of Europe. ▷

The French nation, free, respected by the rest of the world, will bring to the whole of Europe a glorious peace, that will more than recompense the sacrifices that have been made for the last six years. You will return to your homes, and all citizens will point to you, saying proudly 'He was one of our soldiers in Italy!' ▷

Egometer reading
Date: 20-05-1796   Title: Bonaparte   YOU/I ratio: 36

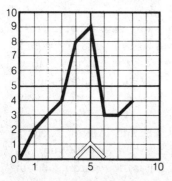

Now compare Bonaparte's speech with the one he made at Waterloo:

Avesnes, 14 June 1815

Men of France:

Today marks the anniversary of Marengo and Friedland, two events which were decisive in deciding the destiny of Europe. Then, like at Austerlitz, and after that Wagram, we were too generous: we believed the pleading sermons and protestations of the princes, and we left them on their thrones! ▷

While today, joined against us, they proclaim their independence and demand the most sacred rights of France for themselves. They are the perpetrators of a most unjust aggression. Let us march forward to meet them: after all, aren't they men, just like us? ▷

Soldiers of France, remember Iena, where, against these same Prussians who today seem so arrogant, you fought and won, one against three. Remember Montmirail, where you were victorious while outnumbered six to one.

Let those of you who were prisoners of the English recite the accounts of their misery and the horrible indignities you were made to suffer! ▷

The Saxons, Belgians, Hanoverians, all the soldiers of the Rhine Confederation tremble, forced to lend their arms to support the cause of the princes, those enemies of justice and the rights of all people. They know that this coalition is doomed. After devouring the 12 million Poles, the 12 million Italians, a million Saxons, 6 million Belgians, they now wish to devour the second ranking states of Germany as well.

They are mad! Blinded by a moment of prosperity. The oppression and humiliation of the French people is beyond their powers. If they enter France, they enter their tomb. ▷

Soldiers, we have forced marches ahead of us, battles to win, perils to escape: but if we remain true to our cause, victory will be ours: we will regain the rights, the honours, the happiness of the homeland.

For all courageous men of France the moment is at hand – to conquer or to perish! ▷

Egometer reading
Date: 14 – 06 – 1815   Title: Waterloo   YOU/I ratio: 16

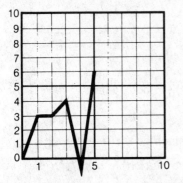

As you can see, the speech delivered on the eve of the Italian campaign scored much higher on the egometer scale than the one which preceded the defeat at Waterloo.

Of course other factors generate enthusiasm and convince an audience, but generally it is safer – except in the case of personal testimonials – to establish a golden word/forbidden word ratio of more than 2, and to make it as high as possible.

A few points to think about. Did you notice in the first speech that it is precisely when he is using the greatest number of golden words that Bonaparte incites his men to act? Did you notice that the golden word curve forms a kind of zig-zag line? This means that you have to vary your effects. Gorging on caviare every day would discourage even the most fervent gourmet. The same goes for golden words.

Putting theory into practice

● Rewrite this passage in order to YOU-ORIENT it:

'When I studied the page in my conference programme where they tell about this morning's keynote session. I noticed something strange. They show a picture of four good-looking men. But they list five speakers!'

'If you studied the page in your conference programme where they tell you about this morning's keynote session, you may have noticed something strange. They show a picture of four good-looking men. But they list five speakers.'

● What introductory technique did Bonaparte use in the first speech?

(1 – personalisation + gripping image.)

● What introductory technique was used in the Waterloo speech?

(2 – news + a fault: being negative [regretful].)

● Compare the two introductions. Read them both out loud to feel the difference.

● What technique did Bonaparte use to conclude the first speech?

(1 – summary + new perspective + quote/citation + identifying.)

● What technique was used at Waterloo to conclude?

(2 – new perspective [not very uplifting = fault] + Doubt [fault] + inciting to [action conquer or perish = doubt = fault].)

● Did you notice that the conclusion of the first speech contains numerous golden words and no forbidden words, while the contrary is true for the second speech?

● Read the two conclusions out loud, adding intonation, to feel the difference for yourself.

How never to be hurt by criticism or objections

People are first and foremost interested in themselves, in other words, not in you. So when they seem to attack you, they are really expressing their own problems.

For example If someone says to you 'Yes, but such a thing never happens in real life! You are wrong!', instead of justifying yourself, ask: 'Do you mean that it never happens to *you* in real life?', and ask the audience: 'Who has already been in such situation? Please raise your hand!' – and then raise your own hand.

The real key, in such situations, is to switch from your own point of view to the point of view of your critic.

> **DON'T TAKE IT PERSONALLY!**
> **PUT YOUR EGO IN YOUR BACK POCKET!**

QUIZ

1. People are first and foremost interested in:
- ☐ **A** The speaker.
- ☐ **B** The theme of the conference.
- ☐ **C** Their business.
- ☐ **D** Themselves.

2. What are the words your audience prefers to listen to?
- ☐ **A** Jokes.
- ☐ **B** The speaker's point of view.
- ☐ **C** You-oriented words.
- ☐ **D** Gossip.

3. How do you avoid harmful critics?
- ☐ **A** Speak louder: cover critics' voices.
- ☐ **B** Don't take them personally.
- ☐ **C** Flatter them.
- ☐ **D** Ignore them.

4. The best combination is often:
- ☐ **A** A combination of introductory techniques.
- ☐ **B** To thank your audience.

☐ **C** To introduce yourself.
☐ **D** A joke.

Answers:
1. D.
2. C: you, yourself, your, yours.
3. B.
4. A.

CHAPTER **12**

HOW TO EXPRESS YOURSELF EFFECTIVELY

'It's not at all surprising that illustrations, when used correctly, add force, vivacity or style to a speech. Because, in addition to their ability to express complex thoughts, each illustration possesses a unique flavour, if I may use the term, which serves to attract attention by pleasing or reaching out and touching the listener.'
DU MARSAIS (1676–1756) French philosopher

'Rhetoric'. What does that word mean to you? A lawyer with tricks up his sleeve? An orator of the last century? It is true that the art of rhetoric goes back a long way (to at least 500 years before Christ). But we also have our own *modern* rhetoric, which we use every day, without knowing it.

Let's start by reviewing what some of the great masters of rhetoric, like Plato, Aristotle or Cicero can teach us.

Aristotle

Aristotle defined rhetoric as the 'ability to discover all possible means of persuasion in a given situation'. And since persuasion depends to a large extent on *proof*, he defined three kinds of proofs.

1. ETHOS. We have already talked about this. It's your attitude, your gestures, your character, your personality, the way you come across. The key word here is *consistency*. If you act, or seem to act, differently from what your words are expressing, then you will not be believed.
2. PATHOS. This is the emotional level of appeal. As a speaker, you should always remember that you are facing normal, *emotional* human beings, and that you must address their hearts and 'guts' as well as their logical minds.

3. LOGOS. Proof through reason. This kind of proof satisfies the intellect, and is achieved through presentation of factual evidence and logical reasoning.

Plato

The main points of Plato's teaching on rhetoric are:

1. *Say only what you believe is true.* We've already seen how 65 per cent of a message is expressed through means other than words, so if you have doubts about what you're saying, they will show.
2. *Organise your thoughts.* We've already covered this point in Chapter 7.
3. *Define the terms that you use.* If a number of interpretations of a word are possible, or if a sentence can be understood in different ways, then remember this:

**Anything that can be misunderstood
will be misunderstood!**

So never hesitate to clarify your thoughts, to give precise definitions to the terms you use ... and make sure you use simple words!
4. *Use correct diction.* We've covered this in Chapter 4.
5. *Practise the art of speaking in public.* It's by practising that you will develop positive habits, and it's those good habits that will make you into a good speaker.

Cicero

Aristotle and Plato were Greek, but Cicero was a Roman. He picked up where his predecessors left off, and improved the art of rhetoric. In his writing we find five areas where rhetoric is applied:

1. INVENTIO. Find your ideas and outline/define the subject.
2. DISPOSITIO. Organise your thoughts. The plan Cicero suggests has six parts: introduction – narration – decision – proof – refutation – conclusion.
3. ELOCUTIO. More than the art of just saying something, this concerns the *style* or the *way* in which it is said.
4 MEMORIA. The techniques of mnemonics applied to public speaking.
5 ACTIO. The practical aspects of the art of expression.

Stylistic devices to stimulate the imagination

While rhetoric used to be an important part of education in times past, it has all but disappeared from the modern school curriculum. Why?

Is it because rhetoric has become an outmoded art? No, since all writers and orators use it, even if they're not aware of it.

Is it because the art of rhetoric has not developed to suit the times? That's closer to the truth, as you can verify when you try to find a simple and practical book on the subject. Such books are very hard to find.

In fact, rhetoric became the victim of its own success. Its techniques have come to be associated with 'smooth operators', notorious for talking a lot without saying anything. It's the eternal question of *form versus content*.

Which of these is more important? If you sacrifice content for form, then you end up with shallow, weak speeches that have no muscle. If you concentrate only on content, then your speech will be dry and uninteresting, no matter how important your ideas may be. As Du Marsais said, 'The art of capturing attention, pleasing and reaching out to touch an audience' . . . has been lost.

So, what are these stylistic devices that we hear so much about? Here's a list of the main ones.

1. Comparison

This is a method of creating a cerebral link between two distant ideas. Imagine, for example, that somewhere in your brain you have stored the image of an Egyptian sphinx sitting in the desert. Someone talks to you about a woman you know. Her name is stored in another part of your brain.

The person says, 'She sat there, like a *sphinx* in the desert.' Bang! The link is established. Whenever you think about that woman in future, the image of the sphinx will always appear at the same time.

You can also try making a strange comparison, followed by an explanation: 'A speech is something like a love affair. Almost any fool can start one, but ending it gracefully calls for considerable skill.'

In order to make a good comparison:

1. *It must be coherent and accurate.* If your comparison is incongruous or exaggerated, you risk achieving the opposite of the desired effect.
2. *The illustration must represent a quality which is more familiar than the real object or person.* Often speakers make comparisons which are too technical, and which only they, and others in the know, can appreciate.

3. *The nature of the comparison must be different from images that we're already used to forming.* One reason why rhetoric became unfashionable was the abuse of clichés like 'strong as an ox' or 'white as snow' or 'pure as the Virgin'. The effectiveness of your comparisons depends on their *originality*.

The key words in a comparison are *like* or *as*.

Do this exercise. Try to find comparisons for:

A. A couch as deep as _____
B. His dry manner of speaking cracked like _____
C. She's as sharp as _____
D. All these men who sacrificed me, who used me like _____
E. Absence diminishes mediocre passions, and increases great ones, like

_____

Here are some suggestions:

A. a tomb (Baudelaire).
B. a whip.
C. a double-edged sword (*The Bible*).
D. an accessory in their lives (Stael).
E. the wind extinguishes candles and ignites fires (La Rochefoucault).

Some other examples:

'The force of selfishness is as inevitable and as calculable as the force of gravity.'
'Business is like riding a bicycle. Either you keep moving or you fall down.'

2. Metaphors

These are a little like comparisons, but here you leave out the 'like' or 'as'. For example, 'A teacher without pupils is a boat with no passengers ...'

Almost any word can become a metaphor: you just have to find a way to introduce an object, person, idea, etc. in an original, striking or unexpected way, by finding another set of persons, objects or ideas which in some way are analogous to the first. In this way, the French politician Clemenceau was called 'the tiger', because there was an analogy between his character and that of a tiger. A very gentle person is a lamb, while someone very strong is a lion, etc. Metaphors are often found in images which are fashionable in society at the moment, so that they can be easily understood.

These days, cars are the source of numerous metaphors: we give someone 'the green light' when we allow them to do something; inflation is 'accelerating', someone has to 'put on the brakes'; people under stress need to 'recharge their batteries', and so on.

To find good metaphors, get into the habit of making comparisons, of looking for associations between words, and just playing with words.

**Make the strange familiar
the unknown known,
the muddy clear.**

If you take my advice and get into the habit of noting down all the images, comparisons, anecdotes, etc. that could perhaps enrich your communication, you will encounter other stylistic devices.

Some examples:

'Profit is the ignition system of our economic engine.'
'Propaganda is baloney disguised as food for thought.'
'What poison is to food, self-pity is to life.'
'A proverb is much light condensed in one flash.'
'An orator without judgement is a horse without a bridle.'
'Sarcasm is an insult in a dress suit.'
'Banker: a man who offers you an umbrella, then wants it back when it starts to rain.'
'A man without judgement is like a car without brakes; but a man without enthusiasm is like a car without a motor.'

3. Personification

Here, objects or animals are endowed with human characteristics: 'This car is out to get me!'; 'This book comforts me . . .'; 'These computers want our jobs'; 'Are commercial banks an endangered species?'; 'As the life-support systems of the economy, financial markets provide a measure of the blood pressure, heart rate, brain waves, and general health of the system'; 'There must be something better England can do to express a diplomatic point than shoot itself in the foot.'

In order to use personification, just imagine that your subject is a human being. What would its character be like?

4. Hyperbole

An intentional exaggeration: 'It weighed a ton'; 'May God strike me down this minute if I'm not telling the truth!'; 'I believe that with the new biotechnology, almost anything that can be thought of can be achieved!'

You can only use hyperbole when you have warmed up your audience enough.

5. Litotes

The opposite of hyperbole, this is a way to express a quality by understatement or by negative phrasing. 'Not bad' (instead of good); 'Not to be overlooked' (instead of important); 'Maybe we can narrow that down just a little bit' (instead of let's see that seriously).

This style is especially useful when you fear opposition from part of your audience.

6. Irony

When you say the opposite of what you mean: 'My kind and generous professor gave me a zero in my exam'; 'This clever business plan which led us to lose so much money . . .'; 'No advertisement has ever bored a reader. That's because it requires little effort and less time to turn the page.'

This is a good way to ruin your opponents' efforts. But be careful: too much irony can also make you enemies and raise opposition from part of your audience.

7. Understatement

A kind of irony, where you say less than what is expected of you: 'I came, I saw, I conquered'; 'I just said a couple of words and he calmed down right away.'

Since this kind of irony is not aimed against somebody else, you can use it freely.

8. Antithesis

A contrast between two ideas: 'They promised prosperity, and delivered misery'; 'What struck me was the visibility of commerce, and the relative invisibility of government.'

Ask yourself what is the contrast between what you have now and what you had before, or what you will have in the future.

9. Periphrasis

Replacing a word by a group of words. Politicians use this device frequently: 'unsatisfactory job opportunities' means unemployment; 'third world developing countries' means poor countries.

10. Climax

An arrangement of words or sentences in order of increasing power: 'A government of the people, by the people, *for* the people'; 'He who loses wealth loses much; he who loses a friend loses more; but he that loses his courage loses all.'

11. Apostrophe

When you speak to a person who is absent: 'Oh, Mr President, if you could only see where you have led us!'

12. Rhetorical questions

A question which doesn't need an answer, or whose answer is implied in the question itself: 'The question is: what can we do about it?'; 'So why, you may ask, do we insist on raising our rates?'; 'How did we get this way?'

Rhetorical questions are very useful to get attention and curiosity from your audience. From time to time, try to work out what kind of objection or question your listener has in mind, and ASK THAT QUESTION, and then answer it.

13. Anacoluthon

A break in sentence structure, to heighten effect: 'Cleopatra's nose, had it been shorter, could have changed the face of the world'; 'The driving force behind any successful business, of any kind, in any country, is the entrepreneurial spirit.'

That gives power to your speech. Well prepared in advance, you can motivate, inspire and fill your audience with enthusiasm using anacoluthon.

14. Antimetabole

Repetition, where the order of the words or the ideas are inverted to produce a contrasting effect: 'Ask not what your country can do for you, but what you can do for your country?' 'This may not, in fact, be a promised land. But it is certainly a land of promise.'

Other examples: 'Medical men say that the radio is useful in certain kinds of deafness. So is deafness in certain kinds of radio'; 'Business is religion, and religion is business'; 'There is no greater fool that he who thinks himself wise; no one wiser than he who suspects himself a fool'; 'Success lies, not in achieving what you aim at, but in aiming at what you ought to achieve'; 'He who fears to suffer, suffers from fears'; 'He who will not when he may, may not when he will.'

Warning

It is most important not to abuse these rhetorical devices. They are much more effective when used parsimoniously. Listen to politicians' catch-phrases. They are often rhetorical figures of speech. The fact that there aren't many of them gives them their strength. (Don't imagine, though, that they happen by accident: there are teams of writers whose job it is to come up with the right figures of speech. Politicians learn them by heart, and then 'slip' them in when appropriate.)

Use action verbs

Verbs express movement, and are better suited to the spoken word than nouns: 'After long reflection, his decision to confess was made' is weaker than 'He reflected for ages, and then finally decided to confess.'

Active verbs are more effective than passive ones: 'You will be amazed by the durability of this instrument' should be replaced by 'The durability of this instrument will amaze you.'

Get rid of the passive:

- is
- has been
- was
- would be
- would have been etc.

when preceding verbs.

How do you transform this passive: 'The department was inspected by the managing director' into the active voice?

The answer is: *'The managing director inspected the department.'*

And what about 'Many decisions must be made by you'?

'You must make many decisions.'

The secrets of efficient language

Do you remember Rudolph Flesch? He devoted his life to improving communication in American businesses and administrations. He gave us our first secret: tell a story. Here are two more.

1. Use short sentences

Listen to people speaking in the street. Their sentences are short. If you attended college and university, you will have acquired a severe handicap: you learned how to *write*, but not how to *speak*. The two are entirely different.

Speaking style is much shorter. When reading, the eye can survey three or four lines of text at a glance, then check back to review anything that wasn't fully understood, etc. This is impossible in oral communication.

**THE LONGER THE SENTENCE
THE EASIER IT IS TO MISUNDERSTAND.**

And I'm not just talking about the people who are listening here. How many times have you heard a speaker lose the thread of his own argument, by getting caught up in long, convoluted sentence structures!

Learn to cut sentences down: take this text and transform the long sentences into shorter ones, injecting them with new life:

Many speakers stay awake all night before their first presentation, and even after years of experience, stage-fright may remain, as was demonstrated by a recent poll that shows that 80 per cent of people are more afraid of speaking in public than of dying; so you're not the only one with stage-fright, a word which is synonymous with fear – there being little difference between fear and courage, since the basis of all courage is fear transformed into action.

The mechanism works more or less like this: fear causes the body to secrete a hormone into the blood, like adrenaline and other known 'stress hormones', substances which are designed to prepare the body for action, by stimulating it and boosting its energy level; and when at such times action is suppressed, the extra energy becomes anxiety; so you must act on the basis of liking your audience, appreciating it and trusting it, because we are not afraid of what we know and like, but rather of what we don't know, which means that you have to learn to approach and appreciate people in order to get over the barrier of fear.

Answer (sample)

How many orators can deny spending nights awake worrying about their first presentation? Even after years of experience, stage-fright can persist. In a recent survey, 80 per cent admitted being more afraid of speaking in public than of dying! So you're not the only one suffering from stage-fright. A synonym for stage-fright is fear. And, in fact, there's very little difference between fear and courage, which can be defined as *fear transformed into action.*

The mechanism works more or less like this: fear causes the secretion of adrenaline and other 'stress hormones' into the bloodstream. These substances prepare the body for action. When the action is suppressed, the extra energy is transformed into anxiety. So you must act, by making an effort to like your audience, appreciate it and trust it. We're not afraid of what we like. We're afraid of the unknown. Learn to approach others and appreciate them, and you will overcome the barrier of fear.

2. Use short words

What applies to long sentences also applies to long words. Short words have more impact. Count the number of syllables, and not the number of letters. You will notice that longer words are often more *intellectual,* while short words tend to be *emotional.*

Here's a list of words, suggested by Herschell Gordon Lewis, an ad. writer. Find synonyms for the words on the left that are shorter, or at least more emotional. First, cover the answers on the right with a sheet of paper.

surplus	more
profitable	good for
competition	challenge
circular	round
terminated	ended
discern	see
experiment	test
perspiration	sweat
to acquisition	buy
selection	choice
sufficient	enough
remunerate	pay
originate	start
ultimate	final

Use lively language

It's a good idea to use familiar expressions, or slang, to stimulate the audience. It's all in the way it's done, which should be both original and tasteful.

Use the *present tense* as much as possible, as well as the *imperative*, and avoid tenses like the past perfect, past conditional or subjunctive.

Also, consider how to use *silences* to your advantage.

And work on your *English*, to avoid common faults.

Create smooth transitions between sections of your presentation, or if you can't, number your ideas: 1, 2, 3, etc.

Here are some short words that are good for transitions:

- Actually . . .
- But . . .
- Who more than . . .
- On the other hand . . .
- What's more . . .
- On the contrary . . .
- In fact . . .
- In spite of everything . . .
- Once again . . .
- Therefore . . .
- And . . .
- For example . . .
- Another . . .
- Now . . .
- A second point . . .
- Here . . .
- Immediately . . .
- In the same way . . .
- Since . . .
- So . . .
- Then . . .
- In other words . . .
- Finally . . .
- Of course . . .
- Similarly . . .

How to stimulate attention

Use phrases to recapture your audience's attention – attention grabbers:

- And that's not all . . .
- It's even better than that . . .

- Wait, the best is yet to come . . .
- But first, you should know a few things . . .
- Now − and this is most important . . .
- And you will see why . . .
- Now you understand why . . .
- But there's one thing more you have to do . . .
- You might be asking yourself . . .
- As you surely know already . . .

But beware!

If you promise something with your attention grabber, make sure you deliver it. If not, you'll soon lose the confidence and interest of your listeners.

Personalise events − give names, dates, facts, precise details, whenever you can.

Do not:

- Use long and complicated sentences.
- Use long and abstract words.
- Lie or try to trick your audience.
- Abuse clichés.
- Use too many figures of speech.
- Hum and haw with words like Well − Hum − I mean − you know −' etc. It's better to keep silent.
- Make grammatical mistakes.
- Talk about banal generalities: 'Everyone knows that . . .'; 'It's been said . . .'; 'It's a well-known fact that . . .'.
- Throw everyone in the same bag by using 'one' or 'they'. 'On the whole, one found the speaker very respectable' or 'Everyone was very happy . . .'. Who is 'one'? Who is 'Everyone'? Always be precise.

QUIZ

1. A comparison should be:
   - ☐ **A** Incongruous or exaggerated, and therefore striking.
   - ☐ **B** Similar to familiar images, so as not to jolt the audience.
   - ☐ **C** The object of comparison should be more familiar than the subject itself.

2. To create a sense of action, you should use _____ (fill in).

3. The two other secrets of action are:
- ☐ **A** _____
- ☐ **B** _____ (fill in).

4. Check the statements which are *true*.
- ☐ **A** You should use the present tense.
- ☐ **B** Better use fillers than remain silent.
- ☐ **C** You should use attention grabbers, even if what follows is not interesting.
- ☐ **D** You should use a transitional remark between each idea.
- ☐ **E** It's better to number your ideas.
- ☐ **F** Intellectual words are useful in order to impress your listeners.

Answers
1. C.
2. Verbs.
3. A. Use short sentences.
    B. Use short words.
4. A, D, E (depending on the situation).

CHAPTER 13

THE ART OF MOTIVATING YOURSELF – AND OTHERS

'Cultivate your enthusiasm like an exotic plant.'
LEON DAUDET (1863–1942) journalist and writer

How to arouse positive emotions in your listeners

It's time to take a look at what we've covered up to now. You've learned how to know yourself better, how to get to know others, and how to recognise – and use – the communication tools at your disposal.

But the most important thing isn't KNOWING, it's DOING.

Now we will be looking at something very important, not only for the Power Talk System, but also in your entire life: ENTHUSIASM.

It's not enough to decide to become an efficient communicator. You need the FUEL to power your boat into the right port. Young newlyweds, salespeople out to succeed, businesspeople, pharmacists, housewives, electricians, everyone needs fuel. This fuel, this petrol, this force that propels us ever forward, is enthusiasm.

So, what is enthusiasm? Write down what you think it is.

Definition of enthusiasm

Here's what my dictionary says: 'Divine transport – intense emotion which leads to joyous action.'

It's a force that makes us resemble the gods and if we are motivated by enthusiasm, we can succeed at anything: no problem, no obstacle, no event can stop us.

Enthusiasm is like a fire that burns all obstacles in its path, that triggers an explosion of activity. Enthusiasm allows you to be creative, to attain something. Education and luck can help, but they're not enough.

Ralph Waldo Emerson wrote: '*Nothing great has ever been achieved without enthusiasm. With it, you can do anything. Enthusiasm can move the world.*'

Consider Abraham Lincoln. He only had one year of primary school before he got into the White House. But the enthusiasm that motivated him smashed all obstacles in his path.

Enthusiasm is a force which powers your entire being towards a fixed goal. Once you have set the goal, you throw yourself, body and mind, into attaining it, and you succeed.

It's this enthusiasm which allows all great men to accomplish their tasks: their own enthusiasm, as well as the enthusiasm they are able to arouse in those around them.

Think about Rembrandt. He dreamed of writing his name in the annals of posterity. He had the luck to meet someone who was impressed with his initial drawings, and who encouraged him to pursue his goal.

Not all of us aim at great achievements in the fields of literature or art. But we all have something to do here on earth. Something more than just having children and bringing them up. We all have a role to play. We are responsible to the society in which we live. We have something important to do in our lives. Every person should be able to say, 'Humanity is a little better because I lived.'

Leave a trace

We also have to instil a sense of enthusiasm in our children, so that they too can accomplish something for humanity. Maybe you think you're too young to do anything important? You forget that Joan of Arc was just 19 years old when she 'expelled' the English armies from France; Alexander the Great led the Greeks to victory at the age of 20; at 25, Napoleon had conquered Italy; Newton made his great discoveries before the age of 25; Victor Hugo wrote his first tragedy when he was 15 years old.

Or perhaps you think you're too old? De Gaulle was President of France at 76. Dandolo, Doge of Venice, led an army at the age of 92! Doctor Johnson wrote his *Life of the Poets* at 72. James Watt learned German in his seventies. Daniel Webster learned 17 languages between the ages of 50 and 70!

All these men left their mark on posterity because of their intelligence, stimulated by enthusiasm. Their ideas led them to a series of actions which in turn led them to success; each new success increased their enthusiasm. They all applied their best qualities to achieving their goals.

What trace are you going to leave? Enthusiasm has no age limits, no sex, no special conditions.

But enthusiasm is not just nervous energy, or exaltation, or getting all worked up. If you're just worked up, you will collapse at the first sign of resistance. *Enthusiasm, on the other hand, is stimulated by difficulties.*

Many authors have had important things to say about enthusiasm. Here are just a few:

'*The success of any great person is due to intelligence, but above all to enthusiasm.*' Dr Pauchet

'*All great historical movements are triumphs of enthusiasm over opposing forces.*' Ralph Waldo Emerson

Nothing can be done without a minimum of enthusiasm.' Voltaire

'*The great accomplishments of man have resulted from the transmission of ideas and enthusiasm.*' Thomas J. Watson

'*Enthusiasm is the thing which makes the world go round. Without its driving power, nothing worth doing has ever been done. Love, friendship, religion, altruism, devotion to career or hobby – all these, and most of the other things in life, are forms of enthusiasm.*' Robert H. Schauffler

'*Nothing great was ever achieved without enthusiasm.*' Ralph Waldo Emerson

Are you enthusiastic?

Would you like to know if you're enthusiastic? Think about each of the following questions, and answer them honestly.

☐ When someone suggests something or makes an offer, do I get carried away?
☐ Do I give up easily in the face of obstacles?
☐ Can I see a project through to the end, even if everyone disagrees with me?
☐ Have I ever been head of a parental, political or professional association?
☐ Am I interested in politics?
☐ Do my friends consider me an enthusiastic person?
☐ Do I see myself as young and vigorous?
☐ What am I planning to do in my old age?
☐ Could I get three or four friends or acquaintances enthusiastic about joining me in taking a Power Talk System oral expression course?
☐ Can I stimulate a group of people by telling them something?
☐ Do I have a lot of friends?

☐ Do I read biographies (of famous people, for example)?

☐ How many times a week do I go out with friends, or entertain them at home?

☐ Who is the most enthusiastic person I've ever met?

Now write down a few lines about your lack of enthusiasm, how it affects your behaviour, and what you plan to do about it.

Human beings need to be enthusiastic. Without enthusiasm, you're old at 25. With it, age makes no difference, and difficulties evaporate. Enthusiasm means having faith in life, faith in your abilities, faith in happiness, and faith in other people.

How to motivate yourself

How can you generate enthusiasm? How can you make it last? First, you have to *want* it. Reading books by and about enthusiastic people can help you, stimulate you and turn you on. One of my favourites is *Success Through A Positive Mental Outlook* by William C. Stone and Napoleon Hill. The title is a good indication of what the book's about: properly channelled thinking can achieve miracles. It is a good companion during those difficult days when your thoughts tend to become morose.

You must also vow never to become an 'extinguisher' of the flame of enthusiasm. And you must also develop that flame, which ignites all great deeds, within yourself. If you do, nothing will be impossible.

You must have encountered these 'extinguisher' types yourself, people who take pleasure in undermining others' enthusiasm. For example, a father says to his son, 'My boy, stop dreaming. It's nice to think about such and such a career, but you have to realise that it just isn't right for you.'

Or the wife who tells her husband, 'Better just let things stay the way they are. You'll have less problems that way.'

Try to become aware of all the subtle, negative suggestions we make, without even being aware of it.

The exterior force of enthusiasm

How can you recognise an enthusiastic person? By their confident walk, their open smile, their determination at work, their intense curiosity. They are self-confident, very sociable, they possess ideals and tenacity. They are not members of the Timidity or Pessimist Clubs.

Every person has the potential for greatness. The enthusiastic person releases this potential from the restraints of banality, mediocrity and routine.

And enthusiasm reveals itself as an exterior force. We've already seen how you can't act directly on someone's inner morale. You have to work on the exterior aspects first, namely the body and its attitudes, in order to get to the inside. So it's by generating enthusiasm in someone, on an exterior level, that you can indirectly influence their interior behaviour. The interior assumes the form of the exterior.

With this in mind, let's do an exercise to generate more enthusiasm in ourselves. It will be like taking a psychic pill. This should be done regularly, since you know that even if you decide to do something, that decision may not have a lasting effect. It must be renewed from time to time.

So first we'll decide to be enthusiastic. And then we'll start tuning our physical attitude, so that our body expresses this enthusiasm. The rest will follow.

Enthusiasm pill:

> **I have decided to be enthusiastic,**
> **and I will act with enthusiasm.**

In future, take this pill at the start of each day: repeat these words, instilling your voice, your head, your hands and your whole body with this dose of enthusiasm. You'll see how enthusiasm can help you change the world, first your inner world, and then the world around you.

An enthusiastic person has the power to influence others

Why be enthusiastic? So that you will be able to fulfil your role in society. You know that an enthusiastic person exerts great influence. We are drawn to such people. Our own influence depends on how much enthusiasm we have. The most difficult test of a person's strength is isolation. Not solitude, isolation. Feeling superfluous and useless is the worst thing that can happen to anyone.

People are meant to be immortal: they should leave works, disciples, followers in their wake . . . We become unhappy when our talents are not wanted, when they waste away inside us, when we bury them for fear of being rejected. A person should somehow mark his or her passage on this planet. By living enthusiastically, by inundating your words and actions with this positive energy, others will be naturally drawn to follow you, becoming your lifelong supporters.

Your enthusiasm can motivate others to do something extraordinary, make them want to understand the secret of your happiness. Through your conviction, they will become a circle of firm supporters. Through your simplicity, you can help them discover the happiness that you yourself are beginning to experience, and make them want to imitate you. Through your ability to communicate, you can make them understand what you yourself have been able to comprehend. Through your sociability, you can encourage them to follow your example.

How to unlock the power of your enthusiasm

Of course, the people around you are no different from people anywhere else: they're not used to experiencing enthusiasm, because in this day and age enthusiasm has become a rare commodity. They are surprised to meet an enthusiastic person.

So tell them your secret. If they don't understand, don't insist. But you should know that there are some people who will be eternally grateful to you for having shown them a way to be happier. So in this way, you can spread happiness around you.

Write down the names of people who you think could benefit from the P.T.S. method, and who you should talk to about it.

This week, set aside a certain time every day during which you will inform others about the benefits of the method. Just to let others know about what you've discovered: a simple way to feel better, and to communicate effectively with yourself – and with others!

So do you feel enthusiastic now? Are you ready to communicate?

The best communication tool

We have devoted an entire chapter to enthusiasm for a very good reason: its astonishing qualities form the basis for the best possible communication tool.

Let me remind you:

● *Enthusiasm liberates.* If you're inhibited by stage-fright, or afraid for any reason, if your ideas are confused . . . enthusiasm will help you get rid of your inhibitions, and help your ideas flow into line. Enthusiasm is a state of *super-lucid creativity*.

- *Enthusiasm provides energy.* It liberates the energy otherwise used for blocking and inhibiting, and allows access to energy reserves that eliminate fatigue and supply incredible strength.
- *Enthusiasm is contagious.* As Ralph Waldo Emerson said, 'Nothing great was ever achieved without enthusiasm.' Enthusiasm is a mobilising force. It spreads like a forest fire, from person to person.
- *Enthusiasm is a skill and not a gift.* Of course, there are people who are naturally enthusiastic. But this quality can be developed. Here's John Green's advice on how to do it.

6 tips for generating enthusiasm

1. Establish an objective, a goal
Without an objective, without something to achieve, you can't be enthusiastic.

2. Improve yourself
Gather information on the subject, think about what you absorb, and *ask yourself questions*.

3. Create an obsession
Have you ever been totally obsessed by some negative idea, maybe a desire for revenge, or a way to humiliate someone? Well, do the same thing, but in a *positive* sense, with your goal.

4. Get your ideas down on paper
Writing is an excellent way of crystallising your thoughts. One idea leads to another, and the challenge of a blank page stimulates the mind.

5. Adopt an enthusiastic attitude
Circulate, smile, let your joy shine through your eyes, speak loudly and clearly so that your heart beats faster. *Decide* to be enthusiastic, and the emotion of enthusiasm will follow.

6. Talk about it whenever you can
It's by talking about it over and over again that you'll find the arguments and conviction to sustain your enthusiasm.

Why don't you make photocopies of the box on the opposite page, and post it where it can be clearly seen both at home and at the office.

ENTHUSIASM

QUIZ:

1. The important thing is not just to know the Power Talk System technique, but to act:
   ☐ Yes.
   ☐ No.

2. What is enthusiasm?
   ☐ **A** An emotion only for immature people.
   ☐ **B** An intense emotion which leads you to joyous action.
   ☐ **C** Something you shouldn't express in front of your audience.

3. What prevents you from being enthusiastic?
   ☐ **A** Being too young.
   ☐ **B** Being too old.
   ☐ **C** Having too many problems.

4. To become enthusiastic, you have to:
   ☐ **A** Read enthusiastic books.
   ☐ **B** Avoid making negative suggestions.
   ☐ **C** Train your body to adopt an enthusiastic attitude.

5. These days enthusiasm is:
   ☐ **A** Common.
   ☐ **B** Rare.

Answers

1. Yes.
2. 'Divine transport' – in other words, intense emotion which leads to joyous action.
3. None of these.
4. A, B, C.
5. B.

CHAPTER **14**

HOW TO GET YOUR AUDIENCE INVOLVED

'Participation, Persuasion and Proof are the three components of conviction.'

STEPHANIE BARRAT

A journalist once said to Elizabeth Taylor, 'You've had many men in your life . . .'. She replied, 'I'd have preferred having a lot of life in my men!' (Note the fine example of antimetabole rhetoric.)

Many speakers also say that they'd like to see more life in their audiences. Retention levels differ: 10 per cent from *reading*, 20 per cent from *listening*, 30 per cent from *looking*, 50 per cent from *listening and looking*, and 80 per cent from *active participation*.

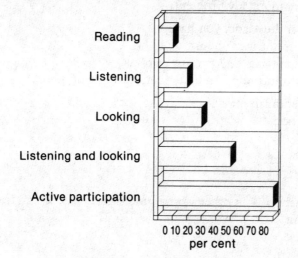

Reading
Listening
Looking
Listening and looking
Active participation

0 10 20 30 40 50 60 70 80
per cent

Retention Levels from Different Activities

How to get your audience to participate

The novice speaker is always hesitant about letting his or her audience have the floor. Who knows? If they're asked to respond, will they have anything to say? Speakers have a great fear of losing control, of seeing an audience get restless, start whispering, shifting chairs, and becoming uninterested.

Actually, just the opposite will happen, if you know how to manage it. By getting your audience to participate:

- You reduce tension because you allow people to act.
- You can use the time to think ahead and to relax.
- You create an atmosphere of warmth and trust which helps bond the group and can make your presentation a success.
- You make your material more interesting and easier to remember.

Questions

There are three kinds of questions: binary questions; closed questions; and open questions. Only the last are dangerous because, unless you set a definite time limit, the person answering has no restraints and may keep on talking as long as he or she likes.

1. Binary questions

Start with these kinds of questions. It's easy:

> *'Who's from abroad? Raise your hand!'*
> *'Have any of you ever encountered this kind of situation? Raise your hand!'*
> *'Who thinks this is a good idea? Raise your hand!'*

The ingredients of good binary questions are as follows:
- You must leave only two possibilities open: raise your hand or not. Answer yes or no. For or against.
- The question must be stated clearly, without room for hesitation or doubt as to its meaning, without ambiguity. Your attitude will determine the reaction of the audience.
- Always follow the question with 'RAISE YOUR HAND!' and at the same time *raise your own hand*. If you just ask the question 'Who thinks this is a good idea?' nothing will happen, and if you don't raise your own hand, you won't get much of a response.
- Use a simple 'Who ...' instead of 'Which among you ...' or 'Are there any ...'. Each member of the audience will feel directly implicated.

This is the ideal type of question to get your audience used to participating. It doesn't require any great courage, or any real involvement on the part of your listeners. It simply gets them to *act*. It can also be used to take a vote, or conduct a fast survey illustrating some point in the presentation.

2. Closed questions (directives)

These questions have only one possible answer:

'What colour are your shoes?'
'What's your line of work?'
'Where are you from?'
'When was the last time ...?'

A. You ask the question.
B. You look at the audience, sweeping the room.
C. You raise your hand.
D. As soon as someone in the audience makes a move or gesture (raises their head, shifts in their chair, etc.) you designate that person (with your hand, not your finger) saying, 'Yes, Sir (or Madam) ...?

This is an *illustrative* technique. If you're talking to a large group, not everyone can answer, but a few people are actively involved, and those who don't reply are *also active* since they are looking for an answer in their heads, just in case they are asked.

3. Open questions (non-directives)

A totally open question can result in answers that are as long as novels! Questions like, 'Why do you love life?' or 'How can we improve our political system?' or 'Why do you believe in God (or not believe)' or 'What's your opinion?'

A partially open question demands more precise answers: 'What are your demands?'

Use these questions in small groups only, where you want to give each participant a chance to express him or herself. You will sometimes have to cut an answer short, because of time limitations.

SET A TIME LIMIT – LIKE A CONTRACT – RIGHT FROM THE START.

'All right, now we'll take five minutes to answer the question ...'. 'You have ten minutes to answer ...', etc.

4. Question periods

Here, the audience asks the questions and you answer. This phase of the presentation usually follows the first conclusion, and should be followed itself by a second conclusion.

It's *dangerous* to plan a series of question periods during your presentation, because every time you let the audience ask questions, you send the ball into the other camp. You risk disrupting the plan of your presentation. This can lead to confusion among your spectators.

Avoid questions while explaining important points. If someone raises their hand to ask a question, write their question down (you will need a paper board), and tell them you'll answer at the appropriate time, at the end of that part of the presentation.

Know how to use questions

When you're taking questions, don't let the interrogators become too long-winded. If they start with a preamble, as soon as they take a breath ask them to formulate the question. Then:

1st Step. Understand the question

One obstacle to communication is *anticipation*. When someone is about to ask a question, people try to guess what it will be in advance, and prepare an answer. Of course, if they do this, they won't really be listening attentively to the question, and won't really listen to the point. So do the opposite: open your ears wide while the question is being asked. Concentrate on listening.

Here, more or less, is how a question works: a person feels some inner tension, something is missing. They ask a question or raise an objection or try to make a point, often unclearly, since they're not really sure what they want to say.

If you have the least doubt as to what they mean, say: 'I don't completely understand. Could you be more precise' or 'Could you explain what you're trying to say more clearly. I don't get the point you're trying to make.'

Here you force the person asking the question to clarify what they want to say . . . and make it *easier* for you to answer.

Don't worry about asking questions to be repeated. Your listeners will appreciate your effort to make things clear. By asking someone to clarify or rephrase a question, you show your consideration and interest in what they have to say.

2nd Step. Reformulate the question

Very often, the question has not been heard by everyone in the hall, and even if you think you've understood it, others may not be clear.

So it's a good idea to reformulate the question, just to make sure that you (and everyone else in the room) understand fully and won't waste time answering off the point.

3rd Step. Accept the limitations of your questioners

Don't say things like: 'You haven't understood a thing!' or 'No'. Instead, start talking with, 'Yes, of course.' or 'I understand your point . . .' or 'I hear you . . .' – *find whatever is positive in the question and restate it.*

4th Step. Use images and examples in your answers

5th Step. Make sure your answer is satisfactory

'Does that answer your question all right?'

Some added advice

- If you don't know, *say* you don't know. Never be afraid of admitting your ignorance. It's much better than trying to cover with vague, meaningless replies that will only confuse and alienate your audience. You may add that you'll look for the pertinent information, or indicate where the questioner might find an answer for him or herself.
- Always tell the truth.
- If a question is long, break it down into smaller units. If there is more than one question, ask which one is most important to your audience, and answer that one.
- Stay calm. Never try to out-voice a member of the audience. Use the rest of the audience to your advantage. If someone persists in shouting out the same question, ask the rest of the audience if your answer was satisfactory, and then get on to another question.
- Be brief and precise. Stick to the *facts*.
- Breathe. Take your time.

9 more ways to stimulate audience participation

While writing this book, we were faced with exactly the same problems that speakers have. How have we stimulated your participation?

- By asking questions (open, closed, etc.).
- By suggesting *exercises*.
- By proposing *experiments*.
- By offering the QUIZ sections.
- By making you *laugh* (sometimes).

So as well as questions, exercises and experiments are two very good ways of getting your listeners to participate.

Here are a few examples.

1. Show the power of visualisation

'Close your eyes and imagine that you're biting into a fresh, tart, acid lemon . . . you all feel the saliva in your mouth . . .'

2. Create ambience, and help your audience get to know each other

'Find someone sitting close to you whom you don't know, introduce yourselves and get to know each other; take five minutes for each person you meet. We'll stop at . . . o'clock.'

3. Reinforce an idea that you've introduced

'Get into groups of two, and ask your neighbour to ask you a question. Reformulate it, obtain his or her agreement, and then answer. Then ask if your answer was satisfactory.'

Placing people into groups of two (or three if a judge or referee is required) is a useful way of conducting micro-experiments with your audience.

4. Movement

Remaining seated and listening to someone talk for an hour is strenuous. Right in the middle of your presentation, you can ask your audience to stand up and repeat the rhyme:

> *'When you're up, you're up*
> *When you're down, you're down*
> *And when you're only half way up . . .*

(indicating everyone who was hiding, who wasn't participating . . .)

> *You're neither up nor down!'*

This will serrate ambiance, make the blood circulate in the veins, and dispel any lethargy and fatigue your listeners might have had.

If you find yourself facing a hall where the first few rows are empty, get the people at the back to move forwards: 'I'm going to ask the people in the last four rows to stand. That's right, stand up!' (Accompany with a gesture.) 'Now find an empty seat down here at the front, and come on down! You'll be able to hear me better, and see the visuals a lot more clearly.'

A great example of audience participation was staged at the Olympic Games in Los Angeles, where each spectator was asked to reach under his or her seat and lift out a cardboard box, which became a piece of a gigantic jigsaw puzzle, representing all the flags of the attending nations. The puzzle was filmed from above, and projected on to a giant video screen.

Any technique you can use that results in gestures or movements from your audience will add life to your presentation.

5. Applause

In a large hall, spectators were asked to applaud on a signal from the speaker, first with one finger, then with two, three, etc.

The build-up effect was extraordinary.

Any time you can applaud someone, do it. Explain why, start applauding yourself, looking at the person, until everyone joins in.

6. Gestures

I don't recommend it, but you must admit that Hitler's salute was an effective gesture.

In table discussions, you can propose toasts (of water) to different people.

Think about the Catholic Mass: genuflection, communion and the sign of the cross, are all excellent ways to get people to participate!

7. Singing

Church ceremonies and tribal gatherings use this technique for getting spectators to participate. But you won't often see people singing at a conference!

On the other hand, more and more political rallies now use singing to get people into the spirit. And, of course, show-business personalities use it to great advantage.

8. Filling out forms

Questionnaires or written exercises which are filled out individually or by groups, and then commented on − even computer terminals (why not?) on which each participant can respond to questions, which are then analysed immediately: these are all excellent ways to get your audience to participate.

Make sure you have a system for distributing documents, which can be cumbersome and take too much time; make sure there are enough pens for everyone; collect the documents when everyone is finished with filling them out, so that people don't sit there reading instead of listening.

9. Stimulate competition

Games, contests and competitions can also be used to promote audience participation.

But be careful not to overdo it, and turn your presentation into a circus or a fair (unless you really are making your presentation at some kind of fair).

Other techniques

What about the following ideas: open-line telephones − a modern way to conduct a question period; hide a document under each participant's chair and make them look for it and fill it out; get the audience to stand up and turn around, in order to see a model placed at the back of the room; make your audience laugh as much as possible? Now it's up to you and your imagination!

QUIZ

1. At the start of a presentation, it's better to:
   - ☐ **A** Ask open-ended questions.
   - ☐ **B** Ask closed questions.
   - ☐ **C** Not ask questions.
   - ☐ **D** Ask binary questions.

2. When answering questions, it's better to:
   - ☐ **A** Anticipate the question, and answer even before the person has finished asking it.
   - ☐ **B** Reformulate the question to make sure that you've understood it correctly.

☐ **C** Minimise the question's importance, so you won't have to answer it.

3. What should you do when you don't know the answer to a question?
   ☐ **A** Say so.
   ☐ **B** Make a note of the question and then forget about it.
   ☐ **C** Say anything in order not to lose face.

4. What are the best ways to encourage audience participation?

Answers
1. D.
2. B.
3. A.
4. Questions;
   experiments;
   movement;
   singing;
   filling out forms;
   stimulating competition.

CHAPTER **15**

HOW TO GAIN DEFINITIVE SUPPORT FOR YOUR IDEAS

'This is the age of scepticism. No one believes anything or anyone. If you say something is the best, you won't be believed just because you said it!'
HERSCHELL GORDON LEWIS, top American copywriter

7 techniques for proving what you say

Many innocent people find themselves in prison because of a misconception they had:

> **'To be believed, all you have to do
> is tell the truth.'**

No! There are some truths which are better left unsaid, and truth without proof is like a captain without a boat.

What better way to stay out of prison than a foolproof alibi? But how many times have people been sent to prison on fabricated evidence, false testimony and confessions obtained under torture − all considered as 'proof' in the courtroom?

To communicate effectively, you must master the art of proving what you say without any doubt.

1. Be precise and explicit

Instead of just saying, 'This is good for active people', which is very vague, be specific: 'You will increase your resistance to fatigue, develop muscular strength, and improve your reflexes.'

If you're describing a pair of binoculars, don't just say, 'With these binoculars, you can see a long way ...', but instead, 'With these binoculars, you'll be able to look a sparrow in the eye at a hundred yards and see him blink!'

You want to tell people how large the book you have to sell is. How would you do it?

Answer: 'More than a pound of ink and paper, 550 pages, 350,000 words that read like a thriller!'

2. Be consistent

The other day, I attended a conference on communication. One of the speakers, John D., outlined the golden rules for good communication – one of them, of course, being to use the first person (I) as little as possible.

Unimpressed with his presentation, I asked myself why. Suddenly, I understood: while he didn't say 'I', he kept on using words like 'my, mine, our, we', etc. The equivalent of thirty-two 'I's in ten minutes.

It was the inconsistency that was the problem. He said one thing, and did something else.

One of the best ways to be consistent is to be honest. Have you noticed how difficult it is to lie? People who lie a lot will often forget what they've said, and then give themselves away, losing the confidence of others for good. Why not simplify life and tell the truth?

3. Present the facts

When I say that Moshe Feldenkrais is a master in the field of personal development, I can back my statement up with proof: 'At 70 years old, he can still pack 5000 people into a seminar any time he wants.'

When I say that negative ions can cure asthma, I back my statement up with: 'Out of 3000 cases, there was only a 10 per cent failure rate.'

And it would be even better to add *who* conducted the study, as well as *where* and *when*.

Proof, proof, proof. It's the basis of our profession. If you can *prove* everything you propose, the end result will be simple: people will be convinced. Without proof, your credibility will be much lower.

What is proof?
Proof is a fact, a date, a number, a name, a place . . . which lends support to what you say. It answers the following questions.

- What proof do I have that this is true?
- Where did this happen?

- Who said this?
- On what authority?
- When did this happen?
- How did it take place?

PROOF IS THE ANTIDOTE OF SCEPTICISM

Make use of titles to lend authority to your references:

'Professor So-and-so of the University of Tel Aviv declared that . . .'.
'On 26 February 1986, the headline on the cover of *Business Week* said . . .'.
'He learned this technique personally from millionaires like Andrew Carnegie.'

4. Quote testimony

There are all kinds of testimony:

- expert testimony;
- celebrity testimony;
- testimonials by users;
- testimony by you;
- anonymous testimonials.

5. Quote the press

People still believe in the printed word. Cut out articles that are related to your subject. Underline passages that could be useful, and quote them in your presentations.

6. Numerical proof

There is an example of numbers used to convince American voters of the need for changes to the abortion laws:

At the present time:
– There is no service, information centre or publicity campaign maintained by the public sector on the issue of contraception. Out of 13 million women of child-bearing age, slightly more than 3 million use contraceptive devices. The law clearly sanctions all propaganda which is in favour of contraception.
– 45 per cent of abortions are carried out on women from poorer

sections of society, especially in rural areas, or from blue collar and/or immigrant families.

– In this country, 315 public hospitals out of a total of 1060 offer free abortions. There are still 15 states where an abortion is practically impossible to obtain.

– What's more, a quota has been set by the medical association establishment: abortions may account for only one-quarter of total surgical procedures.

– Thousands of clandestine abortions are still performed each year (300,000, according to family planning statistics). The M.P.B. (Medical Practices Board) suggests a figure closer to 200,000 per year. These unregulated abortions cause enormous physical and moral mutilation, and sometimes result in accidental death.

Each *fact* is supported by a *number*.

7. Using visual aids to convince people

Visual aids are remarkable tools for convincing people. 'Seeing is believing!' They make your presentations much more dynamic. When preparing visual aids, you will have to review the plan of your presentation, and make adjustments to include the visuals.

They will increase your *self-confidence*, by providing familiar points of reference throughout the course of your presentation, thus making it easier to remember.

Often, visual aids help you feel *more relaxed*: you have something to do, and something to show. While holding your audience's attention, visual aids give you, the speaker, more *freedom of movement*.

When should you use visual aids?

● When you want to help your listeners *remember* or *memorise* something. Visual aids can improve memory by as much as 95 per cent.
● When you're talking about something that your audience *isn't familiar with*: a new product; new procedure; little-known technique; unusual idea, etc.
● When you use *numbers*. In graphic form, numbers 'speak' a lot more clearly.
● When they *prove* that what you're saying is true.
● Whenever they can *motivate* and *convince* your audience.

Which ones?

It all depends on what you want to do. When choosing your visual aids, keep these few rules in mind.

- Only use visual aids when they're *useful*. Don't try to create artificial distractions.
- They should *save time*. If it would be quicker to explain something with words, then do so.
- They should be *interesting* (i.e. that 'which holds attention and captures the mind'). They should be colourful and innovative.
- They should not *break the rhythm* of your presentation. If setting them up takes time, the audience has to remain silent and wait, then their *attention will drop* instead of being heightened.

Which visual aids could you use?

A. The paper stand

Advantages   easy to find; easy to transport; can be used in full light.

Faults   difficult to see from more than 10 yards; rules out the use of photographs; can cause problems (markers that don't work or that are too small, not enough paper, loose screw that falls out when you write, unstable stand, etc.)

- Don't stand in front of what you write.
- Explain what you're writing or drawing OUT LOUD.
- Maintain contact with your audience.
- Use black ink on white paper.
- Press HARD and write with THICK lines.
- Use LARGE letters.
- Finish your drawings.
- Use a lot of fresh pages.
- If you have to make a complex drawing, get it ready before hand.
- If you're working on the bottom of a page and have to stoop over, it is better to sit down.
- You can use this method of visual presentation in combination with others (objects, slides, etc.).

Buy a large roll of paper, or a pad (writing surface should be about 50 × 30 inches) at a stationery store, and prepare any complex diagrams or graphs *in advance*.

If you're worried about forgetting certain points, you can make crib notes on the paper in very light pencil, which will not be seen by the audience. Try to alternate prepared diagrams and graphs with writing text on the spot, to vary your presentation.

If you're going to want to make the same presentation numerous times, you might want to have a graphic artist prepare your diagrams and graphs on sturdier material (cloth, treated paper, etc.) to give your visuals a more professional look.

You can also use sheets of carboard and an easel instead of paper. It's more cumbersome, but allows you to add more visual effects (photographs, colour transparencies, Letraset, etc.). Don't use more than one sheet of cardboard for less than about two minutes.

Make sure that your graphics are visible and easy to read.

B. Transparencies (overhead projection)

Advantages this format allows many kinds of visual effects. You stand *facing your audience*, which means that visual contact is maintained. It looks very professional. It is used by most large businesses and most conference rooms are equipped for it.

Disadvantages lamps burn out pretty often (always keep a spare handy). Adjustments have to be made to obtain clear images. It requires some kind of screen, and is sometimes difficult to use in normal light. Accidents can result in ridicule: text upside down or inverted, images in the wrong order, etc. Spectators must be seated within a certain range in order to see clearly (make sure there are no 'dead' spaces).

- Wash your hands before handling transparencies.
- Prepare your programme in advance.
- Number your transparencies and place them in a file.
- You can prepare excellent transparencies by blowing up slides, newspaper clippings, photographs, etc. on special photocopy machines (in colour or black and white).
- Hide the text with an opaque sheet, and don't reveal an illustration or word until *after* you've presented it orally. Be subtle with your effects.
- If you superimpose transparencies, do it carefully so that they're clear and readable.
- Vary style – colour – content.
- Turn the machine off when you've finished.
- Don't forget: YOUR VISUALS SPEAK LOUDER THAN YOU! So, if you compete with them, you'll lose!

C. Slides

Get them made by a professional. Mediocrity is worse than no slides at all.
Advantages extensive use of photographs; all visual effects possible, in all forms and colours (including superimpositions); the format is very classy, and is easy to handle.
Disadvantages may require an assistant (who may not always be on the ball!); they must be shown in a darkened room (therefore eliminating visual contact with the audience); they can get mixed up (upside down, wrong order, etc.); the projector(s) can cause problems; you need a screen.

- If you use text, choose a classic, easy-to-read typeface (Univers, Helvetica, Times Bold, etc.).
- Don't use a lot of text.
- Don't change the typeface, change the *colour* instead.
- Prepare a title slide, with the name of the conference as well as the names of those who prepared the slide presentation.
- Add a review slide at the end.
- Keep your slides protected.
- Make copies of your slides.
- Organise your presentation on paper first, and co-ordinate it with your overall plan.
- Prepare your slides well in advance (producing a good slide presentation takes at least a month).

D. Graphics

Preparing graphics used to be a complicated process, requiring a graphic artist and a large budget. Today the situation has changed. With the advent of desktop publishing, the use of these indispensable visual aids has become widely available (see page 223). Use them for smaller talks and presentations.

Seeing is understanding. Graphics in the form of graphs and pie clients are an effective tool with which to influence the way your listeners think. Their attention is captured immediately.

- They create an impression of precision.
- They are composed of images, and images are easier to accept as reality than words (seeing is believing!).
- Most of the people you are talking or presenting to do not have the competence to produce graphics themselves, and are therefore impressed by your ability to do so.

● Graphics are associated with serious information, based on reliable sources like a company's financial reports, or scientific data. Their authenticity is therefore not questioned.

E. Other visual aids

● Films
● Video
● Samples
● Models
● Plans/blueprints
● Photographs
● Flashcards
● Objects
● Posters
● Cross-sections.

How to create suspense and add weight to your proposals

The purpose of visual aids is to animate your presentation, to add movement, variety, rhythm. They should under no circumstances *distract* the attention of the participants from your objective. They are simply an alternative, more immediate, means of getting your ideas across.

Always try to use *drawings* instead of text. When you include text, use only key words and avoid complete sentences.

Use the visual aid which is most appropriate for your audience. For 50 people, a paper stand is sufficient. If you have 300 people, you should use a professionally prepared slide or transparency programme.

Don't let your visuals take over: if you distribute photographs, for example, you lose the attention of your audience while they're looking at the pictures. If you leave an image on the projection screen, you will have trouble getting your audience to pay attention to what you say.

Spread out the effects of your visual aids.

QUIZ

1. To be believed, all you have to do is tell the truth.
☐ **A** True.
☐ **B** False.

2. The antidote for scepticism is:
- ☐ **A** To have a positive attitude and self-confidence.
- ☐ **B** To give proof.

3. Visual aids can increase retention by as much as:
- ☐ **A** 20 per cent.
- ☐ **B** 30 per cent.
- ☐ **C** 95 per cent.

4. When you use a paper stand, you should:
- ☐ **A** Face the stand as you write, and stay that way.
- ☐ **B** Remain silent while you write.
- ☐ **C** Use red or yellow markers to *attract attention*.
- ☐ **D** Press hard and write with thick letters.

5. Should your visual aids be directly related to the objective of your presentation?
- ☐ Yes.
- ☐ No.

Answers

1. B.
2. B.
3. C.
4. D.
5. Yes.

PART **3**

How to use professional techniques – and succeed!

CHAPTER 16

WHAT YOU SHOULD DO BEFORE SPEAKING

'Worrying is a non-creative form of imagination which is too often accepted as uncontrollable and normal.'
ALEX F. OSBORN, the inventor of 'brainstorming'

Close your eyes. Now, think about what happens when somebody says to you 'It's your turn to speak.' Try to remember all the thoughts that went through your mind. The excuses you made, the justifications, rationalisations. All the negative thoughts ... and the positive, encouraging ones. We will draw up a list.

The first time we did this experiment, we found thoughts like: 'I'm not ready ...'; 'If I have to do it now, I'll blank out for sure.'

When we ask the same of our students, most of their thoughts are negative:

'I'm shy.'
'I'm not really cut out for this.'
'I know I'm going to screw it up.'
'I'll never be able to do it.'
'I'm afraid of failing in front of others.'
'I don't feel up to it.'
'I don't have the ability.'
'They're all going to laugh at my physical defects.'
'I prefer listening.'
'His trick is really to talk and say nothing.'
'I haven't had enough time to get ready.'
'I'm afraid of making a fool of myself.', etc.

In the A, B, C plan (page 36) that we spoke about, where do these kinds of thoughts fit in? B? Yes, B of course! And what kind of effect do you think this will have on your emotions, and on your subconscious mind?

Now is the time to talk about the subconscious. It has been mentioned often, but do you really know what the subconscious is all about?

How the subconscious works

The word subconscious comes from two words: 'sub' meaning under, and 'conscious' which means will.

The subconscious is therefore that part of our psychic mechanism that operates independently of our conscious mind.

Numerous studies and experiments, carried out mainly in France, the US and Bulgaria, have led to a definition of its main characteristics.

- The subconscious is very sensitive to *suggestion* from others, and to *autosuggestion* (inner ideas or sentences).
- The subconscious is permanently active, day and night.
- It's programmable, like a computer, and if it is not provided with an objective, it will grasp the first objective that comes along, or will adopt *failure* as an objective.
- The 'mental work' carried out on a subconscious level affects not only your thinking, but your entire being, mental as well as physical.
- Precisely because its function is out of your control, the subconscious is *stronger* than the conscious mind.

To understand the subconscious mechanism better, look at the diagram.

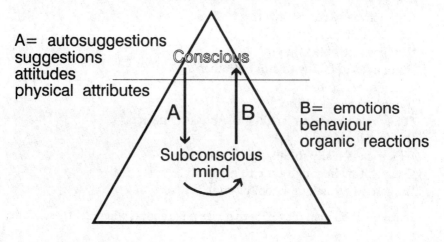

A= autosuggestions
suggestions
attitudes
physical attributes

Conscious

A   B

B= emotions
behaviour
organic reactions

Subconscious
mind

How to fight and overcome thoughts of failure

Imagine the scene. I pick up a glass and a carafe of water. I hold up the glass: 'This is your mind.' Then I hold up the carafe of water: 'This is what you want to say.'

'Look, it's easy: you put the text in your mind, and then you take it out again.' Then I pour the water from the carafe into the glass, and back again.

'Now, look what you're doing.' Saying this, I tear up the sheet of paper covered with our negative thoughts, and stuff the shreds into the glass. With each piece, I read the message: 'I know I'll screw it up'; 'I don't want to make a fool of myself', etc.

The glass is soon full. 'Now look!' I pour the water into the glass, which is full of paper. There's no more room. The water spills out on to the carpet.

'THIS IS EXACTLY WHAT YOU SHOULD NOT DO!'

And I start pulling the pieces of paper out of the glass, one by one, and throwing them as far as I can, shouting:

'I'm full of ideas, I have something important to say!'

'I'm going to be sincere and enthusiastic, and sincerity and enthusiasm are *never* ridiculous!'

'I am gaining more and more self-confidence.'

'If I want to, I can! I will succeed!'

'A lot of other people have done this before. I'm ready!'

'I'm as gifted as anyone else, in my own way . . .'

Now the glass is empty again. 'Now watch closely,' I say, 'you pour your text and ideas into your head . . . and then you take them out again . . . it's so easy!' And I pour the water back and forth between the glass and the carafe.

Have you got the message? This is how we explain it during our Power Talk System seminar.

What to do

Apply the law of substitution, which is the most efficient way to combat doubts, excuses, rationalisations, etc.

When someone makes a negative suggestion, or you make one yourself, fight it and get rid of it by replacing it with its opposite, positive suggestion

What rules should you follow when formulating opposing suggestions?

- Your suggestion should be formulated in the most positive way possible.
- Formulate your suggestions as a progression.
- Make them short.
- Use simple, clear words.
- Make them enthusiastic . . . 'gutsy'.

Doctor Joseph Murphy, author of the bestseller, *The Power of Your Subconscious Mind*, reports the following:

> A young singer was invited to an important audition. She was thrilled and frightened at the same time, because at her last three auditions she'd suffered from terrible stage-fright, and failed miserably.
>
> She had a beautiful voice, but she was sure that when her turn came to sing, she'd panic. In her previous auditions, because of her fear, she'd sung off key and burst into tears.
>
> She worked on overcoming her stage-fright in the following way: three times a day she went off by herself, sat in a comfortable chair, relaxed her body and closed her eyes. When she was completely relaxed, she repeated to herself, 'I sing beautifully. I'm calm, balanced and confident.'
>
> She would repeat these words with conviction, five or six times at each setting, three times a day and once more before going to sleep. At the end of the week, she was perfectly calm and confident, and gave a brilliant audition.

This story illustrates the last key of the Power Talk System method: relaxation.

A relaxation method that gets you ready for action

One of the best things to do is get yourself a cassette. There are a number of excellent ones listed in many mail order catalogues, and available in some bookstores.

Here is the text of a classic relaxation tape. You can tape it for yourself, speaking slowly and deeply:

Concentrate on your right arm ... concentrate all your attention on your right arm ... your right arm is slowly getting heavier ... heavier and heavier ... your right arm is very heavy ... now think: my right arm is so heavy ... my ... right ... arm ... is ... so ... heavy ... heavier and heavier ... so heavy ... completely and totally heavy.

Now do the same for your left arm ... concentrate on your left arm ... your left arm is getting heavier, little by little ... it's getting heavy ... your left arm is heavy ... your left arm is so heavy ... my ... left ... arm ... is ... so ... heavy ... it's heavy ... heavy ... it's completely, totally heavy.

Now shift your attention to your left leg ... it will soon get heavy ... your thigh, your calf is getting heavy ... heavier and heavier ... your right leg is heavy ... your leg is heavy ... now think: my right leg is so heavy ... my ... right ... leg ... is ... so ... heavy ... your right leg is getting heavier and heavier ... it's so heavy ... it's completely and totally heavy.

Now concentrate on your left leg ... relax your left leg ... it will soon be so heavy ... your thigh and your calf are getting so heavy ... heavier and heavier.

Your left leg is now so heavy ... think: my left leg is so heavy, my ... left ... leg ... is ... so ... heavy ... it's very heavy ... completely and totally heavy.

Now your whole body is heavy, heavy, heavier and heavier ... it weighs so much ... it's massive and heavy ... as if you had mercury in your veins instead of blood ... just let your body relax ... completely and totally.

Now bring your mind back to your right arm ... you feel heat in your right arm ... a current of heat ... your right arm is getting warm ... it is warm ... a wave of heat is passing through your right arm ... now think: my ... right ... arm ... is ... so ... warm ... my ... right ... arm ... is ... so ... warm ... it ... is ... completely warm.

Now the wave of heat moves to your right leg ... you feel the heat circulating in your right leg ... your leg is getting very warm ... it is warm ... warm ... now think: my right leg is so warm ... my ... right ... leg ... is ... completely ... warm ...

Now concentrate on your left leg ... you feel the heat already ... it's getting warmer and warmer ... now think: my left leg is so warm ... it's all warm.

You feel the wave of heat moving through your entire body. Your heart is pumping warm blood through your whole body. Your whole body is warm . . . warm . . . and now relax.

You feel relaxed . . . more and more relaxed . . . the relaxation grows . . . it spreads from muscle to muscle . . . into every muscle . . . you are relaxed . . . completely relaxed.

Checklist for 'D-Day'

What you need now is a 'plan of action' to concur with the date you are to make your speech or presentation. See the example opposite.

How to check the room

Telephone the conference organiser. Ask to see the hall. Sit in the audience area to check sightlines and acoustics. Then take the speaker's place, and get familiar with the space.

Introduce yourself to the technicians. Make sure they understand, and can provide what you need. Do they have the kind of projector you want? Is there a microphone with a long extension (or cordless) that can be passed around the audience during question periods? Who is in charge? Will the conference be recorded? Will there be copies available? Could you bring your materials and equipment the day before?

Try to create good relationships with all the personnel. Get some of their telephone numbers, in case of emergency. Call to ask for their advice, assistance, recommendations, etc.

How to prepare yourself mentally

With a clear image of the scene in your mind, it will be easy to make mental run-throughs of your presentation. Get comfortable, relax, and try to *visualise your entire presentation*. Observe yourself in detail:

● your attitude;
● your gestures and use of visual aids;
● listen to your voice;
● audience reaction;
● . . . right up to the final applause. If something doesn't work, START AGAIN.

Conference: 13 March
Subject: Lactic Fermentation and Its Use in Camembert Production

February 1	OBJECTIVE	A single sentence
Feb. 2–9	IDEAS	Let stand 3–4 days
Feb. 10–11	PLAN	Impose limitations, look for proof
Feb.12–14	INTRO-CONCLUSION	Punch!
Feb. 15–25	VISUAL AIDS	Prepare! Very important!
Feb. 26	ROOM CHECK	Go to the hall, talk to people
March 1	MENTAL & PHYSICAL PREPARATION	Dynamic relaxation, breathing exercises, Active Positive Reference Guide, Reference Guide, auto-suggestion visualisation
March 8	RUN THROUGH	Co-ordinate text
March 12	ACCESSORIES	Clothes, documents
March 13	FINAL CHECK	Nothing forgotten?
	R.G. + BREATHING + ACTION!	Go for it!

Do your visualisation as many times as necessary so that the presentation becomes a mental 'routine'.

Concentrate on the feeling of success, of final triumph. Review your Positive Reference Guide feelings (we covered this in chapter 2).

Don't forget to do your relaxation exercises and conscious breathing exercises on page 210.

The cue sheet

All professionals use cue sheets. Just like a driver has a map and a dashboard, you should have your list of cues. Opposite, you will find an example of a cue sheet used in a television programme and on page 172 there is a cue sheet for a seminar on leadership.

The key word here is *timing*. Train yourself, time yourself, pace yourself, and make sure you say what needs to be said in the amount of time allotted.

Always allow for about one-third more time than you plan. Why? Because there are always last-minute complications and unforeseen problems: slight delays; interruptions; setting up equipment, etc.

Orators often lose their notion of time while speaking. When you practise the P.T.S. method, you should become aware of the time passing. Time yourself and set a clock to ring with two minutes left, and again at thirty seconds. When the time is up, you can only add *one* sentence.

Radio and television broadcasters are used to working with these restrictions. They are, after all, only polite. Have you ever had to wait while the speaker before you uses up half your time, not knowing when to stop, thus cutting your question period down to thirty seconds?

In the same way as any job seems to take all the time allotted in which to finish it, a presentation, nourished on verbiage, can go on almost indefinitely! But at the same time, it loses all force and conviction.

Use key words

You should list these '*key words*' on your cue own sheet, as well as the *connecting phrases,* and the whole text of the *beginning of the introduction* and the *end of the conclusion* of your presentation.

Add sketches to represent your visual aids, or use reduced photographs.

Director:	David Bird		Date:	March, 12
Assistants:	Franck Miller/Joyce Hazel			
Producer:	John Hilton	CUE SHEET	Show time:	20.00
Script:	Margaret Wilson	Host: Ian Smith		

MAIN TITLE

HET CPT + DIRECT CAB

1) ALBANIA
2) WINNER

Media	Sound	Minutes	Titles	Writer	Origin
EM	OFF	1	President	Lauderton	BBC
JET		2	Albania	Hall	CNN
DIR		1.30	Postal strike	Van Horn	H
JET		1	New medical discoveries	Bashti	BBC
EM	OFF	2.60	Mini central	Wilkinson	RFO
JET		1.40	Sports for the handicapped	Chilton	ABC
DIR		1	Winner	Addison	BBC

CUE SHEET FOR LEADERSHIP SEMINAR

Day 2   Thursday

Trainers: Ann
          John

Time	Duration	Props & Notes	Content	Trainer
8.00 8.45	45 mins	video	1 *Opening* +exercise A +time for preparation	Ann
8.45 9.15	30 mins	cards	2 *Chain speech* Feedback 2	John
9.15 9.30	15 mins	check time with hotel	*Coffee*	
9.30 10.00	30 mins		3 *Leadership workshop* − reading and vote − divide into 3 teams	Ann and John
10.00 10.30	30 mins		Preparation time	
10.30 11.00	30 mins	video	Exercise part 1	(Ann)
11.00 11.05	5 mins		pause	
11.05 11.35	30 mins	video	Exercise part 2	(John)
11.35 12.20	45 mins	film	Feedback parts 1 and 2	(Ann and John)
12.30			*Lunch*	

Miscellaneous

There are always little details that we tend to overlook: if you have intestinal problems because of nervousness, bring along some appropriate medication. Eat lightly. Make a list of what you need, and make sure everything gets done. We have outlined some comprehensive checklists (see page 195 onwards), which should prevent any major oversights.

If you've forgotten something, improvise. Don't worry. Nobody will notice, unless you tell them about it.

Final advice

If you really can't stop worrying, then ask yourself, once and for all:

WHAT'S THE WORST
THAT CAN HAPPEN IF I FAIL?

You'll still be alive. You can work on it some more. You'll soon forget about it. Put things in perspective. Take a step back and have an objective look at the situation. And persevere!

QUIZ

1. The conscious mind is less strong than the subconscious.
- ☐ **A**   True.
- ☐ **B**   False.

2. When you, or someone else, makes a negative suggestion, you should:
- ☐ **A**   Fight it immediately with an opposite suggestion.
- ☐ **B**   Forget it.
- ☐ **C**   Carry the thought through to its worse scenario, to prepare for everything that can go wrong.

3. Concerning the auditorium or conference room, you should:
- ☐ **A**   Go and check it out the day before.
- ☐ **B**   Check it out on the day of your presentation, when you arrive.
- ☐ **C**   Check it out fifteen days in advance.

4. Visualisation is:
- ☐ **A**   A visual aid technique.
- ☐ **B**   A technique for mental preparation.
- ☐ **C**   A sign at the entrance of the auditorium.

5. Check off the correct statement(s).
- ☐ **A**   It's better to speak for a shorter time than planned, to make room for others.
- ☐ **B**   You should use exactly the time allotted to you.
- ☐ **C**   It's all right to run a little over time.

Answers

1. A.
2. A.
3. C.
4. B.
5. B.

CHAPTER **17**

TELEPHONE TRAINING

'Although everyone these days uses the telephone, the question can be asked why so many people use it badly, why they're not able to get the results they hope for. It's probably because they consider the telephone to be a communication device which allows them to say anything to anyone, in any way they like, and so they don't plan their telephone conversations, keeping the objective they wish to achieve in mind.'

PAUL MAURY

Do you have a telephone? Of course you do. Do you know how to use it? Well, to some extent. But there are a host of ways you can improve your technique, because using the telephone is an art.

By training yourself to use the telephone better, you will communicate more effectively. Carry on reading to find out how.

When Alexander Graham Bell succeeded in establishing the first telephone communication on 10 March 1876, he was probably not aware of the impact his discovery would have on society. Now we can easily reach people on the other side of the globe – or bargain with a shopkeeper down the street without getting up from our couch.

We use the telephone to *communicate* every day. It is, therefore, a perfect opportunity to train ourselves to become more *efficient* communicators. Everything we've talked about up to now can also be applied to telephone communication.

The basic rule of telephone communication

When you talk on the phone, either with a stranger or with someone you know, you only have one indication with which to gauge the reactions of that person: his or her VOICE! Meeting someone face to face is a completely different thing. A whole range of non-verbal signs are available to be interpreted and to help you understand what they mean.

Do they purse their lips in disapproval when you offer them your services? That tells you that the game is far from being won. Do they frown, or take a step back? There are so many subtle signs to indicate disagreement. Do they stifle a yawn, looking embarrassed, or glance at the time? That tells you you are boring them and should hurry up and finish your pitch.

On the telephone, you only have the *voice* to guide you. Therefore, you should develop a quality which is essential to any good communication: the ability to *LISTEN*! To listen very attentively. Listening will enable you to do basic things:

1. To understand the message a person is sending.
2. Find a pertinent response (which, despite the best-laid plans, is not always what you expected).

On the telephone, especially with business calls, silence is golden. It can result in fantastic gains. Why? Because by listening, and letting the other person talk, you learn new information about that person concerning his or her intentions, and eventual objections. So the more other people do the talking, the more they reveal about themselves.

In his book, *Confessions of an Ad Man*, David Ogilvy, founder of one of the largest ad agencies in the world, reveals a secret which enabled him to land many of his important clients:

> There's a strategy which seems to work in almost all cases: get your clients to do the talking. The more you listen, the more they think you know. One day, I went to see Alexander Konff, an elderly Russian who'd made a fortune manufacturing zippers. After showing me his plant in Newark (each room was decorated with zippers two yards long, made for funeral sacks), we drove back to New York in his chauffeur-driven Cadillac. I noticed a copy of the *New Republic* in his hand.
>
> 'Are you a Democrat or a Republican?' I asked.
>
> 'I'm a socialist,' he replied. 'I was very active in the Russian revolution.'
>
> I asked him if he'd known Kerensky.
>
> My client-to-be continued, delighted to talk about his life.

Ogilvy concludes this illuminating anecdote by saying: 'Afterwards, very pleased with himself, the old socialist millionaire told me he'd also known Lenin and Trotsky during their exile. *I just listened, and came away with the account.*'

All good sales people have stories similar to David Ogilvy's. Which means that to be convincing, you not only have to know how to use *words*, but also how to use *silence*.

Silence is important for two reasons: first, you get some insight into what cards the person you're dealing with is holding; second, remaining silent is a subtle way of simply being polite, of paying someone a very effective compliment. By listening carefully to someone, by letting them say what they have to say, you are letting them know that you're interested in them, that you respect them.

In addition your silence can become a kind of mirror (a two-way mirror, since you can see through it) in which clients look at themselves, forgetting their inhibitions and exhibiting surprising enthusiasm.

Because the most important person in the world, in people's eyes, is of course themselves, and everyone possesses an almost irrepressible and insatiable need to talk about themselves. That's why one of the worst things to do in a conversation is to *interrupt someone*. Of course, sometimes there's no alternative, when for example you have to put an end to a conversation, or cut it short because of exterior circumstances (another call, or someone entering your office).

3 ways to get the other person talking

A variation of silence (which can be termed 'verbal' silence) consists of only saying things that will encourage the other person to continue talking, a suggestion which will usually be accepted. You just have to send out signals which confirm that you are listening and interested. These signals can be classed into three categories.

1. Encouragement

'Interesting ...'; 'Go on, I'm listening ...'; 'Yes ...'; 'And then ...'; 'Really ...'; and a range of sounds like 'Mmmhm ...'; 'Ah ...', etc.

2. Understanding

In general, the best way to prove to someone that you understand what they're saying is to *reformulate* their message in your own words.

'If I understand you correctly, you're saying that implementing this method will involve the cutback of personnel?'

'Yes, I see. So according to your figures, it would be better to calculate cost per reader, instead of for the entire production?'

'I want to make sure I understand fully: you've studied the file, and you think that a more modest campaign would be just as effective?'

3. Asking for more details and/or explanation

'Very interesting, but could you be a little more specific?
 'What do you mean when you say that . . .'
 'There's one point I'd like to clear up . . .'
 'What do you mean by that?'

So, especially when talking on the telephone, fight your natural 'ego' instinct to express yourself, and show your maturity by keeping quiet. Even if you've hardly said a word, people will be thrilled to have talked to you, they'll even think you're a brilliant conversationalist!

By the way, this technique works just as well in affairs of the heart as in business. The other person (man or woman) is often looking for love to provide them with an attentive ear, someone they can confide in. Your seductions will be a lot more successful if you listen, instead of putting your qualities and prowess on display.

How to prepare your communication

Obviously, you can't just keep quiet on the telephone, you have to say something. That's why you dialled the number in the first place. But before dialling, *prepare your call in detail,* especially if you want to achieve a precise objective.

For your telephone calls to be effective, expecially in business, they should be prepared with great care. A phone call is a little like a chess move. For it to work, the timing has to be right, and the move well planned. In chess, the winner is usually the one who can best discern the consequences of each move. The same goes for the telephone.

Start by defining precisely the objective of your call. This might seem obvious, yet many people ignore this CARDINAL RULE. Remember that *if you don't know where you're going, you usually end up nowhere.*

To prepare your call properly: take a pen and paper, and write down what you hope to get, or the information you wish to communicate. The simple act of writing things down makes them clearer.

Get into the habit of keeping your notes beside the phone when you make your call. Even if you have an excellent memory, you will almost always forget certain points you wanted to discuss, for the simple reason that conversations often get sidetracked.

Note the points you want to discuss, in the order you want to discuss them. You can even number them. But don't make the list too long, for two reasons.

- First, your listener's capacity to assimilate what you say is limited. If your listener is not in the habit of making notes (as you are, I hope!), then he or she will probably forget half of what you say.
- Secondly, you usually just don't have the time to cover everything on a long list, because the other person has other things to do, other calls to take, clients to see, etc. You don't want to saturate your listener, and detract from the impact of your communication.

So organise the list of issues you want to cover, *in order of importance*. It doesn't matter so much if you aren't able to cover all the secondary points.

And as a general rule, be BRIEF! If you have too many things to discuss, postpone some of them for later. In business, almost everyone is in a hurry.

Being brief doesn't mean you shouldn't get involved in friendly chatting now and then. This can be very important. It adds a personal aspect to the business relationship. Here you should respect the law of listening (it always pays off!). Ask about the other person's health, about their spouse and children, etc. And don't forget about simple, polite manners – introducing yourself, thanking, saying goodbye etc.

As to whether you should engage in this polite conversation before or after covering the essential points, it is often better *after*. First, you don't risk not having enough time to say what you want: your listener will not be forced to put you on hold while you're still talking about the tulips in the park, or a new car. Secondly, by ending the conversation on a friendly basis, you leave your listener with a personal, and therefore attractive, last impression.

When is the best time to telephone?

It might not be easy to know exactly *when to call*, but it is easy to know *when not to call*. In business, Monday mornings and Friday afternoons are OUT. Monday morning at 9:15, and Friday afternoon at 4:45 are the worst times to call.

There are other moments to avoid. If, for example, you know that your client, the editor of a weekly magazine, has to submit his final layout to the printer at 5 o'clock on Wednesday afternoons, then you might not be too well received, and you may even be rebuffed, if you call an hour before. There's always so much to do at the last minute ... changing headlines, running after a journalist who hasn't submitted a text, adding details to ads, etc.

How to end a conversation that drags on

That imperative ring, demanding that you drop everything immediately for what is often an unimportant reason, is one of the more irritating things that we have to put up with in this modern age. So, people who call should be aware that they might be disturbing you ...' wrote P. Camusat in his book *Life and PR*.

This *should* be the case. But unfortunately, most people who call don't bother to ask if they are disturbing you or not. So don't be guilty of this tactless habit yourself. When you call people, make sure they have the time to listen to you. Ask: 'Have you got 3 minutes?'; 'You're not in a meeting, are you?'; 'I hope I'm not disturbing you?'

How to listen

So what happens if someone calls *you*, assuming you have the time to listen. Here are three situations to consider.

1. Someone calls to chat

The rule here is never to be rude and hurt the caller by letting them know that you consider the call a waste of time.

Proceed with *tact* and *consideration*.

Say that someone has just come in, or that you're working on something urgent, or that you're waiting for an important call, etc.

Use circumstances beyond your control as a reason for not continuing the discussion. And if it's true, all the better.

If you are planning to meet the person in the near future, remind them of the rendezvous, and thank them for the call.

2. Someone calls to ask for your opinion

The best thing to do is to *show the caller that you've understood the issue*.
Briefly restate the problem, and then offer your opinion.

If you don't have a clear opinion, say that you'll think about it and call back.

Once you have recapitulated what the caller wanted to say, he or she will feel no need to add anything.

If they persist with small talk, use one of the methods explained in the previous section.

3. You are called to make a decision

Do the same thing here: show the caller that you've understood by *briefly restating* what he or she told you.

Then, make your decision.

If your decision is contrary to what your caller wants to hear, or if you're not sure, say you'll have to think about it and call back.

8 key techniques for answering the phone

Here is a summary of the main points to remember about telephone communication.

1. Express emotion

Emotion is the heart of enthusiasm, and enthusiasm is contagious. Learn to like people, try to see their positive side, think about helping them and express this attitude in your voice, your gestures and in your smile.

2. Smile – be likeable

When you smile, all the muscles in your face relax. There's a relation between the exterior and interior and if you smile, you'll be in a better mood. Your listener can HEAR your smile. Smiling at people says you appreciate and respect them, and is the basis for good communication.

3. Be polite

'Good afternoon, how are you? I hope I'm not disturbing you?'; 'Don't hesitate to call if you have any problems. My name is ...'; 'Yes, I understand ...'; 'Of course, I can understand your point of view ...'; 'I'll do everything I can. You can count on me ...'. Polite phrases like these oil the rusty spots of communicating, even with unpleasant people.

4. Work on your voice

Listen to radio and TV announcers. Try to evaluate them as professionals. Here are a few guidelines.

1. *Isolate each call.* Each person has a unique set of problems. You must be interested in individual cases. Put aside your other preoccupations.

2. *Pause after each sentence.* Give your listener the time to digest what you say.

3. *Visualise an image of your listener.* This will help you smile, express warmth and care, and communicate well.

5. Think about these words

KIND – WARM – COMPETENT – LIKEABLE – SMILING – ATTENTIVE – SYMPATHETIC – OBLIGING – COHERENT – TOLERANT – LENIENT.

6. Don't say NO

Even if you are in disagreement, go along with your caller for a while.

Use phrases like: 'Yes, but ...'; 'I understand how you feel ...'; 'Of course, you're absolutely right, if I were in your position ...'; 'If I understand you correctly ... and what if ... would you be satisfied?'; 'Listen, here's what I propose: ... how does that sound?'

All callers have good reasons for what they say. Try to understand them and, although you may disagree, accept that they have their own point of view ... because they are lacking certain information.

7. Ask questions

Closed questions: 'What amount are we talking about?'; 'Was this a method for hypnosis?'

Open questions: 'Can you just refresh my memory so I can find your file?'; 'What didn't you like about the book?'

8. Use the person's name

'Thanks, Mr X, I hope we speak again.'

Telephone answering machines

'This is a recording. Please leave your name and number after the beep. Thank you.'

Beep! You hang up in a panic. What to say?

Well, here's a good opportunity to practise oral expression, especially the art of improvisation. Take a deep breath, and talk!

Instead of talking to a machine, *imagine you're speaking to the person* who will listen to the message. Speak to that *person*.

It's a good test of your improvisational skills. Without notes, without preparation, you have to get the message across.

ALWAYS LEAVE A MESSAGE IF A MACHINE ANSWERS.

The message on your answering machine

Since I'm often absent − or working on things that demand total silence − I bought an answering machine.

At first, most people hung up without leaving a message. They were probably shy, or thought that what they had to say wasn't important.

To remedy this situation, I erased the 'standard' message that the manufacturer recommended, which was too 'impersonal'. And I replaced it with my own, *personal message*, which created the impression of a dialogue with the caller.

The next week, I noticed a marked increase in the number of messages on my machine. I didn't calculate it, but I'm sure the figure was *at least double* what it was.

Moral of the story: start your message with 'Hello, how are you?' instead of 'This is Mr X ...' or 'This is a recording ...'

Continue, using 'you' to refer to the caller: 'I'm sorry, I'm out at the moment. Please leave your name and telephone number, as well as the reason for your call. I'll get back to you as soon as I can. Wait for the beep ...'

To get the right tone, smile while you're making the recording, and imagine that there really is someone at the other end of the line. *Visualise that person.*

To sum up ...

The telephone is an excellent training tool. You use it constantly. Now, apply all the rules we have covered.

Telephone your own office, or get someone to do it for you, to check on the kind of reception a caller gets.

Use the phone with enthusiasm. Set a precise objective. Be concise and imaginative. Take notes. Be aware of the time, and set yourself a time limit for each call.

When necessary, tape your telephone conversations and listen to them again. Mastering the art of telephone conversation will help you improve your communication in all areas.

QUIZ

1. The first key to effective telephone communication is:
- ☐ **A** Speaking well.
- ☐ **B** Speaking slowly.
- ☐ **C** Listening.

2. To prepare a call, you should:
- ☐ **A** Set an objective.
- ☐ **B** Clear your mind.
- ☐ **C** Do nothing special.

3. Check the statement(s) which are true:
- ☐ **A** You should avoid expressing emotion on the phone.
- ☐ **B** Smiling on the phone doesn't help, because no one sees you.
- ☐ **C** If your caller makes a mistake, say so *immediately*: 'No, you're wrong ...'.
- ☐ **D** If you're not sure about something, *don't ask questions* which might reveal your ignorance.
- ☐ **E** It is impolite to call people by name. Don't do it.

4. The message on your answering machine should:
- ☐ **A** Be impersonal to be effective.
- ☐ **B** Create the impression of a *dialogue*.

Answers

1. C.
2. A.
3. None of these.
4. B.

CHAPTER **18**

HOW TO CONVERSE IN SMALL GROUPS

'The essence of good conversation is not so much saying a lot as letting others discover things for themselves.'

LA BRUYERE (1645–96)

Improvisation training

What kind of public speaking frightens you the most?

If you are like most of us, it's *improvising*.

When do you have to improvise most often?

● When you have to answer questions in front of other people?
● When you want to express your opinion.
● When you're asked to speak, without warning, at a dinner or a meeting.

Are there any other circumstances?

You improve in public every day. During your conversations and discussions, you're always searching for what to say, what to answer . . . in short, improvising.

The art of conversation is a marvellous education. You can practise it much more often than public speaking, and it will sharpen your reflexes and stand you in good stead when you have to improvise in front of an audience.

Dale Carnegie, in his book *How to Speak in Public*, talks about how Douglas Fairbanks used to practise by playing a game for three people – in his case the other two were Charlie Chaplin and Mary Pickford.

Each of us wrote a few subjects for speeches on pieces of paper. We folded them up and put them in a hat. Then we'd each pick one and make a one-minute speech about that subject. We never did the same subject twice. One day I had to talk about lampshades. Try it if you like, and tell me if you think it's easy.

What the game did was to sharpen our minds, teach us a whole lot of things we didn't know, but it especially forced us to get used to organising our ideas and thoughts on any subject very quickly, and expressing them with ease. We were training ourselves to improvise.

Getting started

When you're taken by surprise, the major problem is how to start. You haven't had time to organise your ideas, but you have to start talking anyway!

1. Take time to get started

Each second might seem like a century to you, but each second gives you more time to think. For your listeners, a second is just a second . . . and a short silence at the beginning of a speech is a good way to establish contact.

2. Breathe!

Breathing deeply will inspire you. By replenishing your brain with fresh oxygen you will think more clearly, and stay calm.

3. Avoid abstractions

You will no doubt want to begin by stating your opinions. By doing this, you risk locking yourself into ideas which lack any 'imaginative words'. Start with the CONCRETE. Use what you know:

- that's where you'll find ideas, not abstract ideas, but *concrete* facts and events which you can describe;
- the details you provide will add force to the facts you present to your listeners;
- don't forget to use numbers, dates, pound figures, etc;
- compare things and people with each other, etc.

You will see how much easier it is to describe concrete things: the ideas will flow naturally.

4. Think while you talk

Think about how you will develop your speech. While describing something you are familar with, you can continue *thinking* about what you'll say next, and how you will conclude the speech.

5. If necessary, get the audience involved quickly

You know already that this is an excellent way to gain some time. By asking someone to define a question more precisely, or by asking a question yourself, you give yourself time to think.

What to do if you don't know what to say

Blank. Your mind is totally empty. You're frantic for ideas, but nothing comes. What do you do?

An experienced orator has revealed his secret during a seminar on personal development: 'The answer to the problem of not knowing what to say is simply to DESCRIBE WHAT YOU FEEL.'

And he gave a demonstration during the seminar. He started with these words: 'Hello . . . my heart is beating a lot faster than usual. I'm having trouble breathing, my hands are damp, and I feel you all staring at me. It's like a wave of heat, a vibration that's going back and forth from you to me to you . . . My throat is dry. I'm calming down a little now. The apprehension I felt in my chest is easing off . . .'

He explained that this technique is very useful in situations if you don't know what to say, for example when someone dies, or if a policeman is trying to intimidate you. The simple action of expressing what you feel has a number of consequences.

1. It *liberates* you. You get over the blank space, the block, and are able to continue.
2. It creates a *relationship* between you and your listeners. A mental block can be the result of what is 'unsaid'. The simple fact of speaking re-establishes communication.
3. It is *impossible* to find nothing to say. We always have feelings, impressions or intuitions which we can 'tune in'. Achieving a total mental block is something only a few monks are able to do, and that is only after years of practice!

Don't be afraid of your emotions and sensations. Expressing them will get the audience on your side, unless, of course, you go too far!

One last solution: if you don't know what to say, SAY NOTHING! Silence is also a way of communicating. Concentrate on looking at people, breathing deeply, appreciating the passing moment ...

How to improve your conversations

We have already covered the important factors: listening; empathy; enthusiasm; golden words; sincerity; physical posture; eye contact.

Study the people you're talking to. Think about why they are interesting. Remember David Ogilvy's story from the last chapter.

After each conversation, get into the habit of reviewing it, and evaluating it. What satisfies you about it? How could it have been better?

Re-read the earlier chapters from time to time to refresh your memory.

If you do find faults in your communication, set yourself 'progressive' goals (not ones that are realistically out of reach). For example, you may have the bad habit of clearing your throat at the beginning of your sentences. By becoming aware of it, and working with a tape recorder, you will be able, little by little, to get rid of the habit completely.

Meetings

Many of the rules for telephone conversations apply to personal appointments: set a precise objective; remember who you will be talking to; prepare your strategy and information.

Also, be aware of your appearance ... and get to the meeting on time. This might seem too obvious to mention, but people do slip up.

The first part of a discussion consists of *establishing contact*. You might ask a few simple questions like: 'You had no trouble finding the place?'; 'Have you been here a long time?'; 'This is a great location for an office.'

Then, get right into it: along with the other person, define the *objective* and the *precise framework* of the discussion.

After *concluding*, you might stay a few minutes, thanking your host for the time, the pleasant reception ... just chatting to add oil to any rusty spots that might exist, leaving a positive impression behind you.

Don't forget to make notes and to follow up the discussion by calling back a few days later to see if everything is going smoothly.

Small groups of three to twelve persons

Half-way between conversations and conferences are group discussions. Here, *participation* is very important. Without it, you risk losing your listeners' interest very quickly.

The décor of the room, and the way the chairs are set up, is also important. It is very easy to lose your 'leadership' role when talking to small groups, so every detail counts.

Following are a few examples of how a room can be set up. The leader's place is represented by a triangle, the participants by circles.

The names we have used are only *guidelines*. You can change the set-up as you go along, from one day to the next, for example, to alter the ambience.

Keep in mind that it's always better to have *direct eye contact* with your listeners. So a long, narrow room is not ideal because you won't be able to see the people at the back.

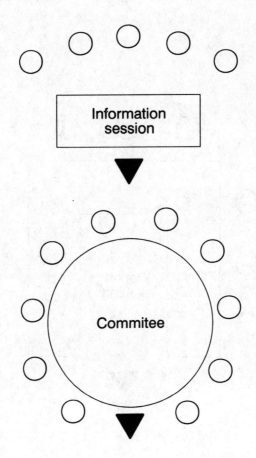

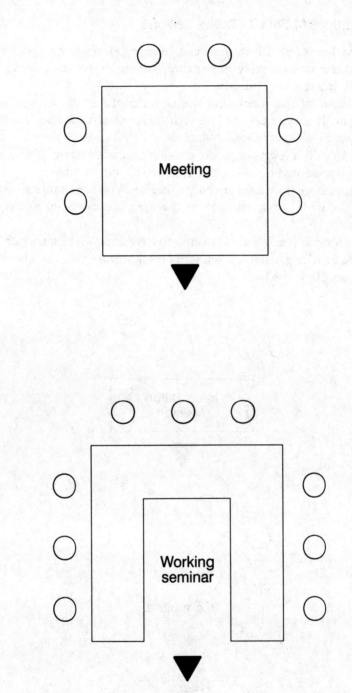

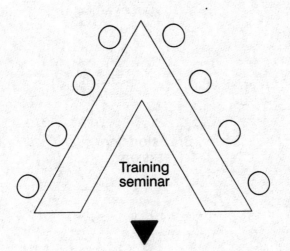

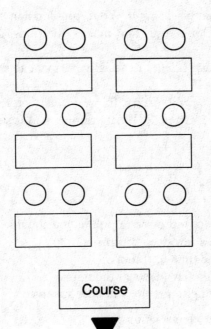

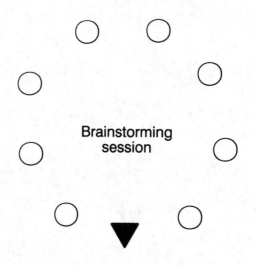

Brainstorming session

What to avoid at a meeting

- *Don't ask too many questions.* Your presentation should not be an interrogation. Don't use too many questions as a pretext for participation.
- *Don't give too much advice.* Especially personal advice, full of 'Is' and 'MEs'.
- *Don't allow long, heavy silences.* Express what you feel.
- *Don't be negative.* 'Oh no!'; 'What you just said is so stupid!'; 'You're wrong ...'.

QUIZ

1. When you have to improvise in public you should:
   - ☐ **A** First take a few deep breaths.
   - ☐ **B** Take some time to think.
   - ☐ **C** Start with a few personal thoughts.
   - ☐ **D** Avoid trying to get the audience involved.

2. To improve your conversations:
   - ☐ **A** It's better to hide your feelings.
   - ☐ **B** It's better to express your feelings tactfully.
   - ☐ **C** It's better not to express your personal feelings.

3. After meetings you should:
- ☐ **A** Call back a few days later, to see if everything is moving ahead as planned.
- ☐ **B** Wait for a call from the person you met.

4. In small groups:
- ☐ **A** A classroom setting is always preferable.
- ☐ **B** A 'U' seating arrangement is best.
- ☐ **C** If possible, a round table is the best set-up.
- ☐ **D** The set-up depends on the circumstances.

Answers

1. A and B.
2. B.
3. A.
4. D.

CHAPTER 19

HOW TO SPEAK IN FRONT OF A LARGE AUDIENCE

'The value of a man can be determined by what he gives, and not by what he is able to receive.'

ALBERT EINSTEIN

The dramatic increase in the number of small radio and cable TV stations in recent years has made it possible for almost anyone to be asked for an interview at some time or other. Companies use in-house videos to communicate information. So it's a good idea to familiarise yourself with studios, TV equipment, sets – and even get to know a journalist.

When you are invited to appear on radio or television, you hold your future, and the future of your business, in your hands. The opinions of millions of television viewers and hundreds of thousands of radio listeners will be based on how you express yourself.

Don't miss this opportunity to become the best communicator you can. Use the advice in this chapter, and your efforts to communicate will be successful.

One day, just before delivering a speech, the person who was to make the introduction asked if she could read excerpts from the letters we'd exchanged before I had agreed to participate in the conference, as a way of presenting me to the audience.

Since I didn't remember the letters at all, I answered yes, without thinking.

She started by reading a letter from her organising committee, offering me exactly *half* my usual fee. She then read my answer, in which I had openly stated (never imagining that it would be read aloud in public): 'Given the fact that I am at least twice as good as any of your usual speakers, I will not accept less than double what you usually pay. When you see my presentation, you will agree that I'm well worth the extra money.'

Having read that, she sat down, and I had to stand up and face an audience which had just been informed that they'd paid *twice as much* as usual, and were ready to kill if I wasn't twice as good!

Isaac Asimov, who published this anecdote in *A Treasury of Humor* (Houghton Mifflin & Co., Boston, 1971) earned a good part of his living as a lecturer.

Maybe you'd like to do the same. If so, you must master the art of speaking in front of large groups.

The art of the microphone

If there are more than a hundred people in the room, it becomes difficult for the average speaker to make him or herself heard. So, it's best to use a microphone or radio mike.

You might be asked to use a radio mike even when talking to smaller groups (twenty to a hundred people), so that the conference or speech can be taped.

Some speakers will insist that there's nothing like the natural voice, and that microphones distort the sound. That may be true, but it is often preferable to use one. Here's why.

1. Your voice doesn't get as tired

If you have to force your voice to be heard at the back, you risk straining it, especially if you're sensitive to air-conditioning systems.

2. Your voice has more presence

All the subtle nuances of your voice can be heard, from whispers to impassioned pleas to forceful commands. You can therefore play with your voice, and benefit from its full range of effects.

3. Improve your voice

For example, you may have a very high-pitched voice. But all you have to do is get the technician to adjust the amplifier, adding more bass, and your problem is solved.

4. You can record yourself

Just ask the technician to do it, or to show you how to do it yourself. Taping and listening to your presentations will help you improve your communication technique.

Some advice on microphones

Using a hand-held mike means your movements will be severely restricted. You will not be free to move around as you'd like. And the wire can be a nuisance. A *clip-on mike*, especially if it's *cordless*, will allow for complete freedom of movement.

Sometimes, the only thing available is a mike on a stand. But make sure that you can detach it and carry it with you when you write on the board, or want to get closer to the audience.

Handle the mike gently . . . if anything goes wrong, there's no more sound!

If something does go wrong, say the mike is too weak, or it isn't plugged in properly . . . then you should be able to do without it. Don't get impatient if it takes the technician a few minutes to solve the problem.

When you hold the mike, keep it under your mouth, so that consonants like P and B don't sound as though they are spat out. You can rest the mike gently between your chin and lower lip. This position will produce excellent sound, and the distance between the mike and your mouth will always be the same, which is not always the case when holding a mike by hand.

Don't forget that mikes pick up ALL sounds. If you have to swallow or burp or cough, hold the mike away.

Remember that mikes do not add enthusiasm or life or force to your voice. On the contrary! They tend to even out the sound.

How to set up the room

A mike may carry your voice to the back of the hall, but your eye contact is still dependent on the set up of your lectern *vis-à-vis* the seating arrangements.

Look at the examples on the next few pages. The black triangle represents the main speakers and the circles represent the audience or other conference members.

For panel conferences:

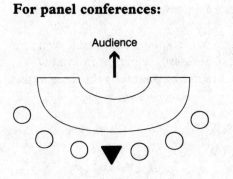

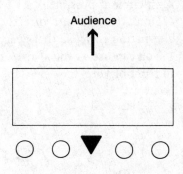

For a speech or presentation:

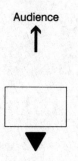

desk facing the audience . . .   or to one side

For a symposium:

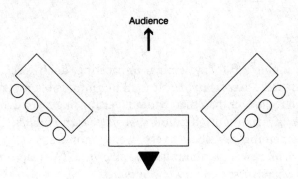

The audience itself should be seated in rows with lateral aisles, in a semi-circle if possible.

Don't place chairs directly behind one another: shift them over, in alternating rows, so that everyone can see past the person in front.

You can use a central aisle, but you might be put off by the 'hole' right in front of you.

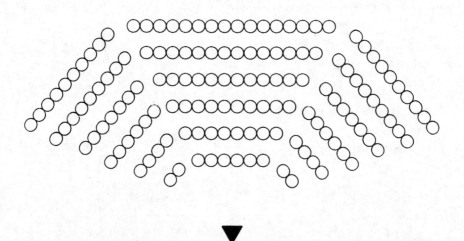

Smoking is usually prohibited in large auditoriums. If not, ask your audience: 'Which of you don't smoke?' Some people will raise their hands. So, politely ask the others to wait for the pauses and go outside to smoke.

Taking breaks

If you are running a full-day seminar or meeting, don't forget to plan a pause *at least every ninety minutes*. It is all but impossible for an audience to stay seated for longer than that, without getting fidgety or disinterested.

The cycle of maximum attention span is *twenty minutes*. So plan to introduce something new about every twenty minutes.

Further, plan a twenty-minute period like in a TV soap opera: there should be a *climactic event every four minutes!*

How to be a strong leader

An audience not only has to be surprised regularly, it also has to feel that the speaker is a leader.

If your audience is apathetic, shake it up. If it's hostile, stay calm, ask people with questions to express themselves clearly, and answer them clearly (see Chapter 14).

Your self-confidence and leadership are expressed in your voice and attitude. A firm, poised tone and correct posture will help assert your role. Pay attention to what you do with your hands and arms. If they move freely and openly, you will be more in control of the situation. If you feel restricted, if you cross your arms or hands, you will express fear, and your public will feel it.

When there are sixty or more participants, the audience starts to react like a single entity, and not like isolated individuals. This collective organism is much more sensitive to emotion, and tends to stick together. Beware the speaker who attacks one of its members!

Here's a mnemonic to help you remember the qualities of a good leader:

Language – imaginative

Empathy

Attitude – positive

Direction

Enthusiasm

Repetition

Imaginative language

Motivates people, can be understood by all, stimulates memory and leads to action.

Empathy

Sensitises you to your public, makes you aware of subtle reactions, and helps you adapt your presentation to suit your audience's character.

Positive attitude

Helps you deal with problems, instils hope in your audience, and through physical posture, expresses self-confidence.

Direction

If your goal, towards which all your efforts are directed, is not perfectly clear, then you will not attain it, and neither will anyone else. If, on the other hand, your goal is precise and clearly formulated, then you will be able to lead your audience to it.

Enthusiasm

The key to your inspiration, magnetism and power over others!

Repetition

Use it both in *repeating things you say*, and in *preparing* your presentation by visualising each detail in advance.

How to speak on radio

Here's a situation where your audience seems large, but really it isn't. Because each person listens to the radio *as if it were speaking to them alone*.

Since the audience is very heterogeneous, it is impossible to adapt your style to a target group. Just talk simply, articulate well, and try to put some warmth and life into your voice.

Summarise what you're talking about regularly: people might be listening while driving, or doing something else and they might have missed the introduction.

Use short sentences and short words. Make frequent efforts to retain the audience's attention: it's a lot easier to shut off the radio than to get up and walk out of an auditorium.

Time your conversation. Each second counts, and you cannot run over time. Be aware of your timing.

As one regular broadcaster says: 'Radio doesn't intimidate me, because no one sees me. I can be sitting in the kitchen, dressed the way I like, hair uncombed, etc. I experience no stage-fright because I'm not afraid of forgetting something. I can read my notes, while on television you always have to be looking at the camera, or at the host.'

Appearing on television

First, watch the programme that you're invited to appear on. Observe its format – the possible PITFALLS and advantages.

When you appear on TV, you have to be aware of your 'image'. Wear colours that look good on the screen. White, for example, looks bad. The lights produce too much reflection. Blue is much better, as are all pastel colours.

Be careful about jewellery that can flash and disturb the viewers. Glasses should also be avoided, unless they're anti-glare. If possible, wear contact lenses.

If you haven't just returned from vacation, looking tanned and healthy, get a good rest the day before, and think about your make-up: a white skin doesn't look good under the lights, so you should get an artificial base, not too much, not too little.

The intense lighting may disturb you. Nevertheless, try not to blink.

Think about visual aids. They are particularly effective on TV, but they have to be professional.

You can refer to notes on the radio, or even read from a written text, but when you are on television the only thing you can rely on is a prompter, with essential headings (or a small card with your main points).

Control your movements, and slow down. If you don't, the camera won't be able to follow you. Moving around too much distracts the viewers.

When you've finished, *don't get up* until you're told to. Usually, titles, will be superimposed while you and the host continue chatting.

What you should not do

- Don't appear tired.
- Don't wear white or black clothes, or dress tastelessly.
- Don't smoke.
- Don't perspire because you're too hot.
- Don't look around, instead of at the person to whom you're talking.
- Don't cross your legs.
- Don't make a lot of nervous gestures.
- Don't speak in technical jargon.
- Don't use long sentences.
- Don't forget to smile.
- Don't speak to a *mass of people* – rather, pretend you're speaking to a small group.
- Don't get carried away.
- Don't think you're on a podium.

QUIZ

1. Microphones:
- ☐ **A** Are useful, are not very practical.
- ☐ **B** Are generally useless. Better do without them.
- ☐ **C** Are very useful.

2. The best way to hold a mike is:
- ☐ **A** Right in front of your mouth, very close.
- ☐ **B** About 10 inches from your mouth.
- ☐ **C** Resting lightly, between the chin and the lower lip.

3. It's best to take a break at least every:
- ☐ **A** 20 minutes.
- ☐ **B** 30 minutes.
- ☐ **C** 90 minutes.
- ☐ **D** 120 minutes.

4. On the radio, it's better to talk to the listeners:
- ☐ **A** As a large audience, to give them that 'group spirit'.
- ☐ **B** As individuals.

5. On television:
- ☐ **A** Visual aids are useful.
- ☐ **B** Visual aids should be avoided.
- ☐ **C** Visual aids are prohibited.

Answers:
1. C.
2. C.
3. C.
4. B.
5. A.

CHAPTER **20**

HOW TO IMPROVE YOURSELF

'There are two types of people who never amount to anything in this world: those who can never do what they're told, and those who can only do what they're told.'

ALBERT EINSTEIN

4 ways to make progress

A real professional is someone who is always trying *to learn more.*

To do this, there are a number of tools at your disposal.

1. Your own observations

Watch speakers on television. Cut the sound − or cut the picture. When you attend a conference or a speech, make notes. Keep a file on 'effective communication' which contains any interesting methods and effects you come across.

Record yourself, and listen to yourself (or watch yourself on video). Find out what you've got going for you, and what you should try to improve.

2. People's comments

Ask participants to fill out an evaluation form whenever possible. Get friends and colleagues to attend, and ask for their opinions, remembering that if they are true friends, they will tell you *everything* they think:

'There's no better mirror than a true friend', says a Chinese proverb.

3. Attend a training session

As good as it is, no book can fully replace a live public speaking seminar. It cannot compensate for full weekend training sessions, hours of watching yourself on video, and the practical aspects of participating in group situations. The energy of the group helps you improve. You will refine your perceptions of others, and of yourself.

4. Expand your reading

We've already recommended *Success Through A Positive Mental Outlook*, and at the end of the book you will find a complete bibliography.

Interviews in magazines can also be a source of interesting and useful information. Learn how others deal with questions, supply proof for their statements, introduce and conclude a subject, use visual aids, etc.

Use the checklists

The following pages include 'checklists', which summarise the entire Power Talk System method. Refer to them regularly.

Whenever you have to make a presentation, you don't have to carry the entire method with you. Just prepare the appropriate checklists.

The main causes of failure and the solution

Albert Einstein's remark, which opens this concluding chapter, illustrates perfectly the possible reasons for failure.

If you don't want to follow the advice offered by this book, then you will deprive yourself of dozens of years of experience, and will have to 're-invent the wheel' all over again, despite the fact that it's all here already. You will waste a lot of time.

But, if you ONLY follow our advice, then you risk not finding your own style. Your personal touch will make your communication original, and your originality will strengthen the power of your performance.

The solution? Read and re-read the book. Open your eyes and observe the world, the people in it . . . and yourself!

The power of suggestion

One of the main causes of mental block lies in negative 'suggestions' and the inhibitions they produce. You should therefore pay particular attention to the following tendencies.

1. **Comparing yourself with others.** This is the best way to drain your self-confidence. You are unique. Accept yourself as you are, with your qualities and faults, and change yourself gradually.

2. **Wanting to be perfect.** Here, you compare yourself to an ideal image of yourself. Since you *cannot be perfect* (nobody's perfect!), you will be disappointed, and once again lose self-confidence.

3. **Being afraid of rejection.** This visceral fear, experienced first as a child who is afraid of losing its parents, on whom it depends totally, often stays with us into adulthood. You won't be rejected because you're not perfect. And if some people do reject you, *don't take it personally*. It's *their* problem.

4. **Not praising yourself.** An excellent form of autosuggestion is to acknowledge your own qualities and strong points, and to encourage yourself. Many people think that you can only learn from your mistakes. That's not true. You can learn just as much from success, if not more.

Your future

> *I look to the future, because that's where I'll be spending the rest of my life.*
>
> Charles S. Kettering, a colleague of Ford

The future looks bright for communication. Technology is advancing: with cassettes, video, satellite, computers . . .

And who is to control all this? Who feeds the computers with ideas? Who produces the videos?

Communicators.

As sophisticated as the technology gets, the essence of communication remains the same. By mastering the art of the spoken word, you will gain a definite advantage over those who work with the written word alone. You will be understood by *everyone*, whether you write or speak. Your communication will be interesting and forceful.

The Power Talk System might just be your key to fantastic success. But you must give it some time and energy. You now have the tools. It's up to you to ACT! Remember this thought from Maslow:

**'EVERYTHING YOU CAN BE,
YOU SHOULD BE.'**

CHECKLISTS

Checklist No. 1

Eye contact:

☐ accentuates what you say;

☐ is always directed at the people you're talking to;

☐ if you have to read a text, practise using the TV announcer technique (see Checklist No. 8);

☐ an attentive gaze is a precious tool that helps you see and *control* everything taking place around you!

Voice:

☐ lively and confident, your voice is a manifestation of your self-assurance;

☐ vary the volume, pitch and rhythm of your voice;

☐ make use of silences;

☐ BREATHE correctly!

Posture:

☐ try to remain balanced at all times. Feet well planted on the ground (even when seated), shoulders relaxed, arms and legs uncrossed. This posture allows your body to move freely.

Gestures:

☐ your gestures should be naturally full and smooth and accentuate what you say;

☐ be your best visual aid.

Checklist No. 2

Preparing for D-Day

☐ Have you transformed your notes into 'conductor' files?

☐ Practise remembering ideas and key words instead of memorising texts by heart.

☐ Practise speaking out loud – use intonation and other effects for emphasis. Imagine that each rehearsal is the 'real thing'.

☐ Use your visual aids!

☐ Time yourself. Gradually cut your time down. Don't forget that in reality things always go more slowly, so add one-third of your total practice time for the real presentation time. That's right, one-third! It's better to run a little short than too long, and risk ruining your conclusion.

☐ Think about your body language (see Checklist No. 7).

☐ Rehearse in front of an audience, and listen to their comments attentively.

☐ Tape yourself a couple of times on a tape recorder, or better still with a video camera.

☐ Listen to and/or watch yourself, and take notes using the self-evaluation sheet provided on page 209 (photocopy and enlarge for your personal use.)

☐ Do a dress rehearsal – wear the outfit you'll be wearing on D-Day.

☐ Rehearse, but don't lose your spontaneity and flexibility.

Checklist No. 3

Questions for organisers

☐ What are the dimensions of the auditorium?

☐ How will the room be set up? Will spectators be able to take notes?

☐ Is there any way you can improve the set up?

☐ What audio-visual equipment is available?

☐ Is lighting available? Can lighting be installed?

☐ If so, insist on having a technician present.

☐ What about the microphone? (See Checklist No. 6.)

☐ What time do you start your presentation?

☐ For how long will you be speaking?

☐ Are there other speakers before you? After you?

☐ How has the schedule been organised and who is in charge?

☐ Who's in charge of organising equipment and materials?

☐ At what time will the auditorium become available?

☐ Is there a podium or stage? Is there adequate lighting? Will you have a table?

☐ Will there be any breaks or intermissions? When?

☐ Will refreshments be served?

☐ Will you have a telephone available? Who takes your messages?

☐ Who will be greeting members of the audience?

☐ How is the auditorium ventilated?

☐ What colour is the background you'll be standing in front of? (Your clothes shouldn't clash!)

☐ How is the room temperature controlled?

Checklist No. 4

You may have to read out a text, without being able to change even a single sentence (a scientific report, a financial report, a political declaration, a speech written by someone else, etc.). If so, do the following.

☐ Start by reading the text over a few times out loud – get used to pronouncing the words.

☐ Practise the TV host technique. Delivering a written text well depends on your eye contact. Look at the text and read a part of a sentence in your mind. Then raise your head and speak that part of the sentence while looking at your audience. Read the rest of the sentence silently, then look at the audience and speak the rest of the sentence, etc. Only speak when looking at the audience. Read in silence. You can practise in front of a mirror. The technique should become a habit.

   You will be able to read texts with more expression, and to maintain eye contact with your audience. It also helps you to avoid reading too fast.

Checklist No. 5

What you should do just before speaking

☐ You've taken a walk and breathed in plenty of fresh oxygen.

☐ You stopped practising the night before.

☐ You've eaten a light meal (you need your blood in your head, not in your digestive organs!).

☐ You haven't taken any alcohol – you've been drinking water or juice instead.

☐ Talk to the organisers of the event, and the people in charge of the auditorium, the equipment (you've already told the technician what s/he has to do – see Checklist No. 3). Get these people on your side.

☐ Check all your equipment is working properly (e.g. slide projectors). If you're using a drawing board, do you have enough paper? Enough markers? All the colours you need? Do they all have enough ink?

☐ Adjust the microphone. Do a sound check.

☐ Take a seat at the back of the auditorium and make sure you can see.

☐ Check to see if there have been any last-minute changes to the programme.

☐ Make sure all your documents are in order. Always make a photocopy of your conductor's plan and keep it with you at all times, especially if you have to travel!

☐ Make sure your visuals *are* visible and readable from everywhere in the room.

Checklist No. 6

The microphone

☐ Keeping your voice level up for any length of time in a room with more than fifty people is very tiring so use a microphone.

☐ Allow enough time to adjust the microphone.

☐ Make sure a technician is there during your presentation, to re-adjust the level with the audience present, and to help you out in case an emergency arises.

☐ Find out how to turn the mike off. Never speak to someone in private with the mike on – you never know who's listening!

☐ If possible get a cordless clip-on mike, which allows you almost complete freedom of movement.

☐ If the auditorium only has a conventional stand mike, try to obtain (or improvise) a 'dog collar' and attach the mike around your neck. Always be aware of the wire!

☐ Avoid standing or fixed mikes. They nail you to one place!

☐ A microphone increases the volume of your voice, but does nothing to enhance expression. Double your enthusiasm!

☐ Practise speaking without a mike – you never know when an equipment breakdown may occur.

☐ Should the curtains be drawn?

☐ Listen! Are there any distracting noises? A construction crew outside? Muzak? Another conference next door? Try to eliminate them.

☐ Check the temperature of the auditorium – if it's too warm your audience will fall asleep!

☐ Find a private corner where you can do some dynamic relaxation exercises to put yourself in touch with your body.

☐ Walk back to the auditorium with a smile and greet the audience as they arrive.

☐ This is no longer the time to think of yourself. YOU are not important – only what you say and do!

Checklist No. 7

On your marks, get set ... GO!

☐ Breathe.

☐ Remember that people SEE you before they HEAR you.

☐ If someone introduces you, listen attentively to what they say about you.

☐ If you have to cross the auditorium to make your entrance, do it calmly, walking purposefully to the podium. Breathe!

☐ As you get comfortable and take possession of your space, look at your audience and smile. Find your 'balanced' position. Centre your breathing. Count 1–2–3 in your head.

☐ The audience becomes silent and attentive. You are in control. Breathe.

☐ Give your introduction some PUNCH!

☐ Remember: be flexible! The unexpected is always possible, and you have to be ready to deal with it. Having a good 'conductor' plan, regular practice, and a precise awareness of time passing, are all effective tools for adapting rapidly to new situations.

Checklist No. 8

Radio and television

Journalists are usually so used to what they're doing that they forget to give you some very basic instructions. Here's what you should know when talking to a journalist or TV interviewer.

☐ A good journalist will hear and use everything you say. So don't reveal any 'confidential' information, thinking it will be kept off the record.

☐ Ask for a list of questions the journalist intends to ask you beforehand (but still be prepared to answer other questions).

☐ Find out what kind of programme you'll be on – Humorous? Documentary? News?

☐ Will there be any other guests?

☐ Find out if the journalist wants short or long answers.

☐ Journalists are usually in a hurry, so get to your interview on time.

☐ Make sure you watch a broadcast of the programme you're going to be interviewed on beforehand.

☐ Get to know the journalist's particular style.

☐ Don't worry if the technicians on the set seem to be having fun. They're not laughing at you!

☐ Say a few words to the technicians. Ask them a couple of questions about their work. It's much better to have them on your side than against you.

☐ Let the journalist lead the interview, but interrupt politely if s/he rephrases what you say incorrectly. Remain in control. You are the guest!

☐ Never lie.

☐ Always stay calm and avoid any direct conflict with the journalist.

☐ Always remember why you're there (a good journalist will usually remind you).

☐ Never forget that journalists need information, and it's up to you to help them do their job!

☐ Be wary of using highly technical language.

☐ Don't be shy about insisting you understand the question. A precise response to a well understood question is much better than a vague answer to a question you didn't fully understand.

☐ Choose: there are some interviews which you should absolutely refuse to give.

☐ Time is critical: 30 seconds of TV time costs a lot. Watch your watch!

Checklist No. 9

The telephone

Making appointments:
☐ always start by repeating the name of the person you're talking to;

☐ introduce yourself;

☐ explain the reason for your call;

☐ don't say too much;

☐ suggest two possible meeting dates;

Sales:
☐ be prepared;

☐ set an objective;

☐ get motivated, and be confident;

☐ listen − try to discern the person's specific needs;

☐ stay calm and positive;

☐ transform negative responses into advantages. Ask 'Why?';

☐ ask concluding questions;

☐ close the sale.

Breaking off calls:
☐ tap on your table, as if someone were knocking at the door. Excuse yourself and hang up.

☐ keep a tape recording of a telephone ringing. Turn it on, excuse yourself and hang up.

☐ to screen calls, pretend you are the receptionist.

Checklist No. 10

Choice of Conference Location (Venue)

	Bad	Medium	Good	Comments
Access				
Parking				
Signs				
Cloakroom				
Reception				
Sales booths				
Toilets				
Public telephones				
Dimensions of the room				
Shape				
Obstacles (columns, etc.)				
Windows (careful about glare)				
Ventilation and heating (adjustable?)				
Organisation of the auditorium				
Placement of tables and chairs				
Writing materials?				
Acoustics				
Ambient noise (music through non-soundproof walls, construction, kitchen noises, etc.)				

	Bad	Medium	Good	Comments
Audio visual equipment available – paper or blackboard – slide/film projectors – rear view projectors – screen – markers – P.A. sound system				

Can the lighting be adjusted?

What kind of microphones are available?

Is there a technician?

Can the speaker be seen from everywhere in the room?

Is the podium well lighted?

Jugs of water on the tables?

No telephones in the auditorium

What time does the auditorium become available?

Any other events happening at the same time?

Intermissions – When?

How long?

Where?

Who takes messages?

Who's in charge of phone calls?

_____

No smoking sign

_____

Name and telephone number of person in charge of the auditorium

_____

_____

Name and address of the technician

_____

_____

_____

Cost in relation to planned expenditure

_____

_____

_____

_____

Checklist No. 11

Plan for preparing a presentation

Date of presentation _____ Duration _____.

Place _____ Time _____

Subject _____

My objective _____

Participants _____

	Deadline	Done
Researching information		
Sorting information		
First draft		
Let it sit		
Visual aids − 'Attention grabbers'		
Audience participation methods		
Prepare the introduction and conclusion		
Second draft		
Organising equipment		
Translating manuscript into 'conductor' files		
Preparing answers to questions		
Testing the presentation		
General rehearsals		
Psychological preparation: anti-stage fright		
Just prior to D-Day: Physical relaxation exercise		

Checklist No. 12

Control list

Hotel or building:
- ☐ Location
- ☐ Parking
- ☐ Transportation
- ☐ Exhibition facilities (sales booth, info kiosk, etc.)

Auditorium:
- ☐ Shape
- ☐ Comfort of seating
- ☐ Colour (avoid red)
- ☐ Windows (can they be masked?)
- ☐ Acoustics
- ☐ Model
- ☐ Noise
- ☐ Reception area (for intermissions)
- ☐ Electric outlets
- ☐ Writing boards
- ☐ Tables
- ☐ Air conditioning
- ☐ Interior lighting
- ☐ Proximity of kitchen, restaurant, etc.
- ☐ Bar (paid by participants during intermissions)
- ☐ Meals
- ☐ No telephones in the auditorium

- ☐ Notify secretary
- ☐ Notify photographer

Sound equipment:
- ☐ Tape recorder
- ☐ Speakers

- ☐ Cassettes
- ☐ Microphone (multi-plug)
- ☐ Extensions

Visual equipment:
- ☐ Projectors
- ☐ Spare lamps
- ☐ Slides
- ☐ Screen
- ☐ Cardboard graphics
- ☐ Writing board
- ☐ Markers

Diverse:
- ☐ Scotch tape
- ☐ Penknife
- ☐ Screwdriver
- ☐ Scissors
- ☐ Pliers
- ☐ Printed placards
- ☐ Kleenex

Entrance table:
- ☐ Books and/or cassettes
- ☐ Change
- ☐ Cash
- ☐ Documentation of other events
- ☐ Bibliography of the presentation
- ☐ Blank paper
- ☐ Pens
- ☐ Subscription cards
- ☐ Files

Communication Evaluation

Date_____ Title _____

Duration _____

Subjects analysed	Page No	Points (circle your score)				Comments and evaluation advice	Score
YOU							
EYE CONTACT	55	0	15	30	50		
SMILE	180	0	3	6	10		
VOICE: rhythm	50	0	3	6	10		
articulation	49	0	6	13	20		
volume	48	0	3	6	10		
vitality	51	0	6	13	20		
POSTURE	58	0	15	30	50		
LOOK	61	0	6	13	20		
SUBJECT MATTER							
INTRODUCTION	84	0	20	40	60		
PLAN	79	0	20	40	60		
BACK-UP	151	0	12	25	40		
VISUAL AIDS	154	0	15	30	50		
TRANSITIONS	131	0	3	6	10		
GOLDEN/ FORBIDDEN WORDS	112	0	12	25	40		
IMAGE WORDS	123	0	12	25	40		
SHORT SENTENCES	129	0	3	6	10		
PRESENT TENSE	128	0	3	6	10		
TIMING	170	0	12	25	40		
CONCLUSION	91	0	20	40	60		
YOUR PSYCHOLOGY							
AUDIENCE INVOLVEMENT	142	0	23	45	70		
EMPATHY	103	0	30	60	90		
SYMPATHY	101	0	10	20	30		
ENTHUSIASM	134	0	30	65	100		
GOALS ATTAINED	64	0	30	65	100		
						YOUR TOTAL TOP SCORE	1000

APPENDIX

BREATHING TECHNIQUES

Breathing is the basis of oral expression. The expulsion of breath is directly related to the creation of sound.

- Filling the brain with oxygen > memory lapse = inspiration!
- Regular deep breathing = massages the solar plexus (the centre of emotions), stomach breathing.

We breathe naturally. But we can also learn how to breath consciously and centre our breathing so that we feel its effects and gain maximum benefit from them.

Proper breathing means breathing deeply and calmly, soothes mental agitation. This is a reflex you should acquire. Take advantage of the affects of deep breathing by walking as much as possible. At the office, practise deep breathing a number of times every day. Breathing with your stomach helps you get to sleep.

1. Start by breathing out through your nose. Straighten your back without tensing up. Slowly empty your lungs. Now breathe in through your nose, calmly, deeply, slowly. Think about what you're doing, feel the changes occurring in your body as you breathe in fresh oxygen. Now breathe out slowly. Repeat the cycle two or three times.

2. Lie down flat on a couch or carpet and place your hands on your stomach. Now breathe in and out deeply, filling your stomach with air and emptying it, feeling it rise and fall under your hands. Imagine that your stomach is a balloon which is slowly being filled with air, and then emptied. Never force too much air in!

3. Now place your hands on the lower part of your rib cage, under your chest. Place them flat on your moving ribs. Breathe in and out calmly, slowly, and feel your ribs move under your hands. Your rib cage expands with each intake of breath, and contracts as you breathe out. Concentrate solely on your breathing, and on the sensations it produces throughout your body.

4. Now breathe only by filling the upper part of your rib cage. Imagine that the air entering your lungs is raising your shoulder blades. Keep breathing calmly and slowly, and concentrate only on your breathing.

5. Stop concentrating on your breathing. Let yourself breathe naturally, and relax.

6. Concentrate again, and resume your deep breathing, filling first your stomach, then your lower rib cage, and finally the upper part of your rib cage. Do a few breathing cycles, and feel the sensation of calm pervading your entire body.

Your mind plays an important role in this exercise. Try to evoke images that represent a state of calm and rest for you, and which are also a support for correct breathing.

'Soothing your mind through appropriate movements neutralises muscular tension. When the mind is soothed, your entire body feels relaxed.'

HUEI NAN TSU

HOW TO USE COMPUTER GRAPHICS

Computers even make better graphics than before, since what you do appears instantly on the screen, and changes can be made to increase the impact and persuasive power of the graphics you produce.

First let's take a look at a very simple graphic, made with Digital Research's 'Gemgraph' program (IBM compatible). For an example, let's say you have to transmit the following numbers during a presentation on mail order and inflation.

Enter the numbers in your computer, press a button and you get the following options:

MAIL ORDER
Fuelled by inflation?

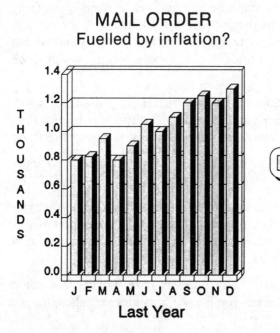

MAIL ORDER
Fuelled by inflation?

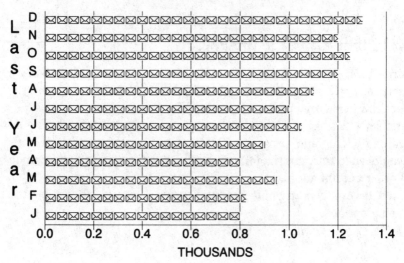

MAIL ORDER
Fuelled by inflation?

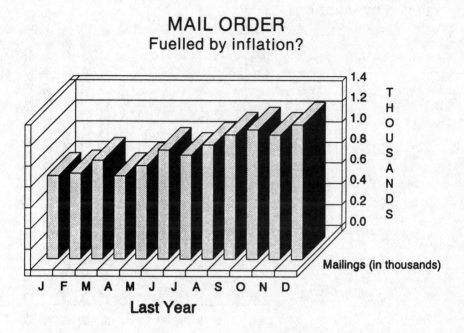

J F M A M J J A S O N D
Last Year

Mailings (in thousands)

MAIL ORDER
Fuelled by inflation?

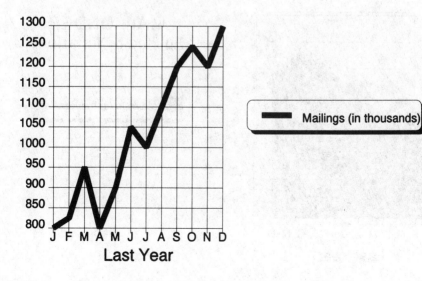

J F M A M J J A S O N D
Last Year

Mailings (in thousands)

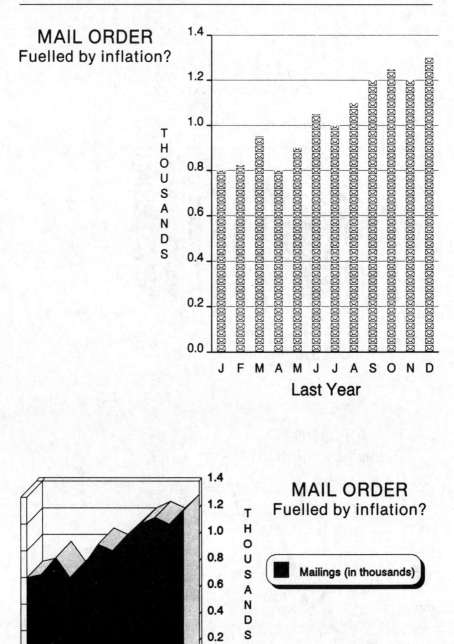

MAIL ORDER
Fuelled by inflation?

Last Year

MAIL ORDER
Fuelled by inflation?

■ Mailings (in thousands)

Last Year

Which graphic will you choose?

It all depends on what you want to say, and who you're talking to. Let's look at all the different kinds of graphics, starting with the simplest and most common form:

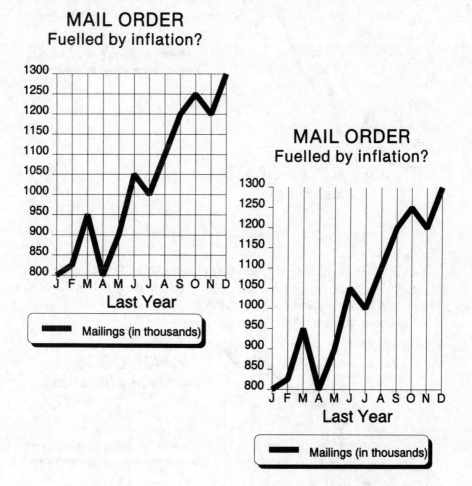

'Not much you can say about it . . .' you may be thinking. Not true. Even this simple graphic can be used to communicate various subtle pieces of information, and help prove what you are proposing. But you have to know how to make it 'power talk'.

In your presentation, perhaps, time (here represented by months passing) is much more important than amounts of money. If you get rid of the horizontal lines (see above right), the months will stand out!

If it's the amounts you want to emphasise, get rid of the vertical lines.

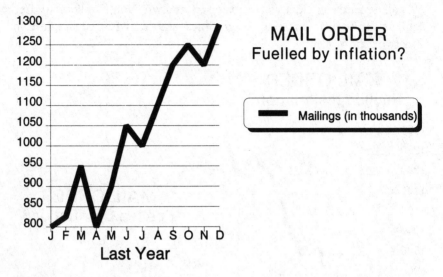

See the difference?

Now let's say you think the curve rises too quickly and contradicts what you're trying to say — i.e. that the country or company is behind in its production standards and could go faster.

What about this graph?

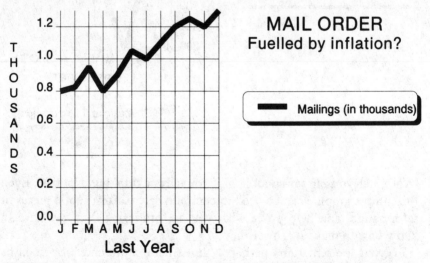

This time we simply changed the initial value. Instead of taking 0.8 as the starting point, we start at 0.

You can do more to enhance the image of slow or fast growth by using graphic tricks. For example, if you add horizontal markers to your line, it seems to rise more slowly.

On the other hand, if you fill the curve with vertical markers, the line seems to climb more rapidly. Compare the two graphs: they are identical.

Adding lines to your base chart will have the same effect.

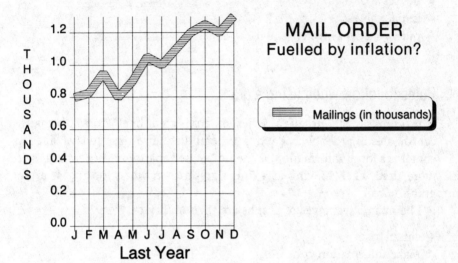

MAIL ORDER
Fuelled by inflation?

Mailings (in thousands)

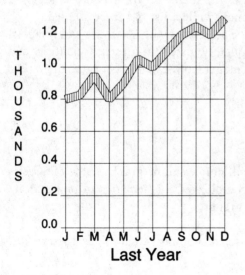

MAIL ORDER
Fuelled by inflation?

Mailings (in thousands)

What conclusions can be drawn?

Although graphics appear to be objective, they are not. They are tools that can be used to improve your presentation.

It's your task to make them work for you – talk for you – by manipulating:

● the scale of data;
● initial values;
● purely visual aspects.

Rules to follow when using a graph

The graph made up of a series of connected lines drawn between coordinates is probably the oldest type of diagram in use today. Since it contains a lot of information, it should be used sparingly. It's easier to get more tired when looking at a linear graph than when looking at a pie graph.

The main advantages of graphs are their ability to:

● summarise;
● make information coherent;
● add interest;
● create impact;
● increase credibility;

If you compare a graph to a list, you'll see that the graph provides you with all the information at a glance, while a list has to be studied.

In the reader's mind, graphs are associated with scientific and financial studies. Because they are frequently used to present scientific and financial data, they are therefore more credible than other types of graphic representations.

Using graphs in presentations

For presentation purposes we will only examine graphs made of a series of lines. Curves require more complicated mathematics to plot and are more difficult to read than line graphs.

Let's take an ordinary graph.

If we want to emphasise the form and not individual values, then we just eliminate the background.

MAIL ORDER
Fuelled by inflation?

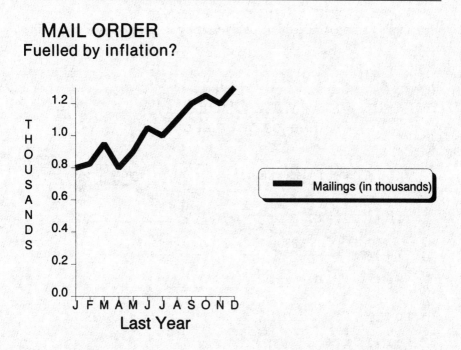

If, on the other hand, we want to make reading the values easier, then we simply add a grid:

MAIL ORDER
Fuelled by inflation?

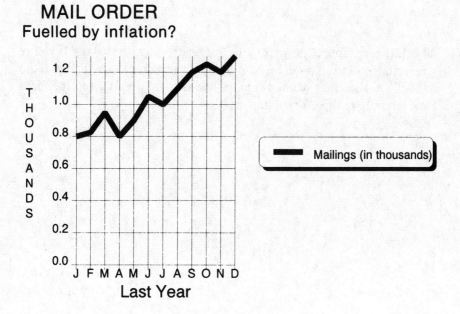

We can also emphasise each value by writing it in above where the line breaks:

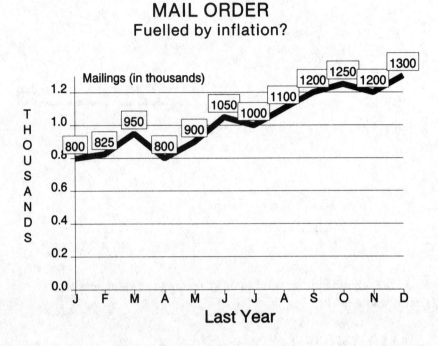

MAIL ORDER
Fuelled by inflation?

The thicker the line of the graph, the less readable are the values. If you're just trying to show a trend, then a graph with a thicker line will have more impact. On the other hand, a smaller line is more precise, and therefore looks more scientific. Try it and see!

Use pie graphs to explain and persuade!

If you intend only to glance at this page because you think graphs aren't for you, then read the following text and look at its subsequent graphic representation:

In a survey of investment clubs it was found that 20 per cent of club members were between 20 and 34 years old, 42 per cent were between 35 and 49 years old, 30 per cent between 50 and 64, and the remaining 7 per cent were over the age of 65.

INVESTMENT CLUB
Division of membership according to age

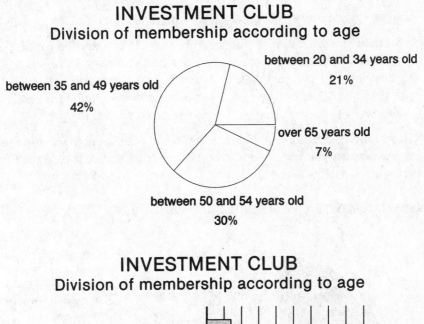

between 20 and 34 years old
21%

between 35 and 49 years old
42%

over 65 years old
7%

between 50 and 54 years old
30%

INVESTMENT CLUB
Division of membership according to age

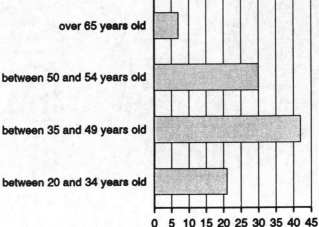

When should you use a pie graph?

Use a pie graph when you want to compare a number of elements to each other AND in relation to a whole.

If you compare the same information expressed as rectangular blocks to a pie graph, you see that the bars are more precise in comparing elements to each other, but that the pie graph is much more effective comparing elements to the whole.

An important precaution

How would you show the following information?

> Breakdown of investment club members: 13 per cent small business owners, 12 per cent professionals, 2 per cent students, 13 per cent employees, 33 per cent business executives, 11 per cent with no profession, 12 per cent retired, 2 per cent agriculture and 2 per cent diverse.

If you use a normal pie graph, then you won't have room to write in the professions. So you have to add a key, and design different patterns for each value.

Breakdown of investment club members

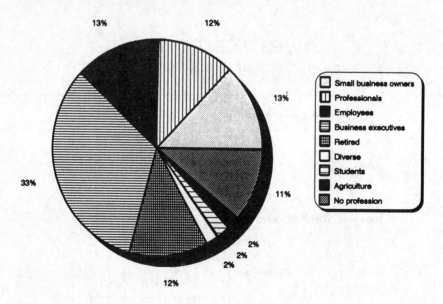

But even after you do this, there's a problem. What is it?

Answer There are so many elements that some become almost indecipherable!

This leads us to one of the fundamental rules of using pie graphs:

> **Never include more than 6 elements**

If you have more, as in the previous example, then show only the six main elements, and include the others under the 'diverse' heading. If necessary, you can break down the 'diverse' category in a second graph.

Breakdown of investment club members

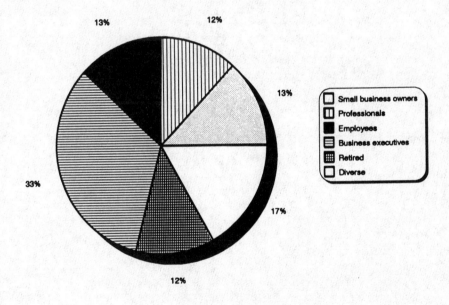

How to make your pie graph more attractive?

The first way is to add a *pattern* to each part. If you are able to use *different colours*, all the better!

Another method is to add *depth* and give your chart a 'shadow' (as in the example).

If you want to emphasise one of the elements slightly, separate out one *wedge* from the others.

You can also comment on each element by *isolating* it from the rest in turn.

As you can see, graphs are a real science! Next time you use graphics, think about your objective, and design the graphs accordingly.

BIBLIOGRAPHY

Blohowiak, Donald W., *No Comment! An Executive's Essential Guide to the News Media*, Praeger, 1988

Carnegie, Dale, *The Quick and Easy Way to Effective Speaking*, Pocket Books, 1970

Conger, Jay and Rabina Kanungo, *Charismatic Leadership*, Jossey-Bass Publishers, 1988

Cowan, Robert, *Teleconferencing: Maximising Human Potential*, Reston Publishing, 1984

Dunckel, Jacqueline and Elizabeth Parnham, *The Business Guide to Effective Speaking*, Kogan Page, 1985

Fast, Julius, *Body Language*, Pan Books, 1972

Godefroy, Christian and John Clark, *The Complete Time Management System*, Piatkus Books, 1990

Maltz, Maxwell, *Psycho-cybernetics*, Pocket Books

McCarthy, James S., *Public Speaking*, Monarch Press Inc, 1965

McCarthy, James S., *Speech*, Monarch Press Inc., 1965

Murphy, Herta and Herbert W. Hildebrandt, *Effective Business Communications*, McGraw-Hill, 1990

Quick, John, *A Short Book on the Subject of Speaking*, McGraw-Hill, 1978

Reed, Warren H., *Positive Listening*, Franklin Watts, 1985

Sarnoff, Dorothy, *Speech Can Change Your Life*, Dell, 1970

Sorrels, Bobbye D., *Business Communication Fundamentals*, Charles E. Merrill Publishing Company, 1988

Steckel, Robert C., *Profitable Telephone Sales Operations*, Arco Publishing Company Inc., 1976

Stone, William C. and Napoleon Hill, *Success Through a Positive Mental Outlook*, (originally published as *Success Through Positive Thinking*), Thorsons, 1990

Watson, Dunn S., *Public Relations*, Irwin, 1986

Weitzer, Skip H., *Telephone Magic*, McGraw-Hill, 1987

Westland, Peter, *Public Speaking*, Hodder, 1983

Thill, John V. and L. Bovee Courtland, *Excellence in Business Communication*, McGraw-Hill, 1991

INDEX

absent person, speaking to 115
abstractions, avoiding 174
abstract style 32
abstract words 120
accents 36
action
    audience, involving in 74
    fear as preparation for 13–14
    inciting in audience 82–3
action verbs 116
active participation by audience 29, 74,
    130–8
Active Positive Reference Reserve
    18–21
advice, giving 180
aggression 11
Alexander the Great 123
Allport and Postman 29
ambiance, creating 131, 135, 136
anacoluthon, use of 115
anecdotes, personal 75, 84
anger 47
anticipation 133
antimetabole, use of 115–16, 130
antithesis 68, 114
anxiety 13
apostrophe 115
applause 136
appointments, making by telephone
    202
apprehension 13
Aristotle 109–10
arms
    crossed 46
    freeing 46
articulation 37–8, 110
Asimov, Isaac 183
attacks, dealing with 24

attention
    capturing 28–9, 72–8
    span, maximum 186
    stimulating 119–20
attitude 10
audience
    attention span 186
    checklist 207
    collective entity, as 187
    empathy with 91–2
    evaluation of performance by 191,
        196, 209
    getting to know one another 135
    interest in, showing 11, 89, 90,
        100–8
    interest of, sustaining 67–70, 89, 90
    involving 74, 130–8, 175
    large 182–90
    leadership 187–8
    listening to 10, 11, 89, 90
    making them feel important 89, 91
    movement by 135–6
    needs of, meeting 89–99
    objectives, setting 53–5
    participation by 29, 74, 130–8
    retention levels 130
    small groups 173–81
    tension, reducing 131
auditive oriented people 43–4
auditorium
    controlling 45
    dead space 45
    noise and silence 28–29
    seating arrangements 45, 185–6
    and setting objectives 53–5
    temperature 197
    see also room setting; venue
authenticity 11

Piatkus Business Books

Piatkus Business Books have been created for people who need expert knowledge readily available in a clear and easy-to-follow format. All the books are written by specialists in their field. They will help you improve your skills quickly and effortlessly in the workplace and on a personal level.

Titles include:

Presentation and Communication
Better Business Writing Maryann V. Piotrowski
Confident Conversation Dr Lillian Glass
Confident Speaking: how to communicate effectively using the Power Talk System Christian H. Godefroy and Stephanie Barrat
He Says, She Says: closing the communication gap between the sexes Dr Lillian Glass
Personal Power Philippa Davies
Powerspeak: the complete guide to public speaking and presentation Dorothy Leeds
Presenting Yourself: a personal image guide for men Mary Spillane
Presenting Yourself: a personal image guide for women Mary Spillane
Say What You Mean and Get What You Want George R. Walther
Your Total Image Philippa Davies

For a free brochure with further information on our complete range of business titles, please write to:

Piatkus Books
Freepost 7 (WD 4505)
London W1E 4EZ

PIATKUS

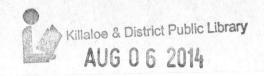